WORDS FOR LIVING

WORDS
FOR
LIVING

An Anthology of Meditations for different Moods and
Seasons, but mainly for late Evening.

by

DOUGLAS AITKEN

Illustrations by
Barbara Ann Hall
and Carol Summers

THE SAINT ANDREW PRESS : EDINBURGH

First published in 1983 by
THE SAINT ANDREW PRESS
121 George Street, Edinburgh EH2 4YN
Copyright © Douglas Aitken, 1983
ISBN 0 7152 0519 6

Printed in Great Britain by
CWS Printers, 35 Bogmoor Place, Glasgow

TO FIONA

who has encouraged me with love and patience through dark and light, storm and peace, for more than twenty years and without whom I am certain I would be lost.

ACKNOWLEDGEMENTS

Since these meditations were almost all written for broadcast in a slightly different form from the one in which they appear here, I have to pay tribute to those producers, all colleagues or former colleagues of mine, who have taken my rough scripts and knocked them into shape. In my rewriting of them for this book I have remembered the lessons I learned from the Rev. Stewart Lamont, now a prolific writer and broadcaster living in Edinburgh; Father Bill Anderson, now Spiritual Director at the Scots College of the Gregorian University in Rome; Father Willie McDade who still shares an office with me in the BBC in Edinburgh; and the Rev. Donald N. Macdonald, now minister of St. Columba's Church, Glasgow. To all of them, and all the secretaries who looked after us and still do, and who typed the scripts and timed the broadcasts, my grateful thanks.

Scripture quotations are taken from the Good News Bible, published by the Bible Societies/Collins, © American Bible Society 1976; The Living Bible, copyright 1971 by Tyndale House Publishers, Wheaton, Ill. Used by permission; New English Bible, Second Edition © 1970 by permission of Oxford and Cambridge University Presses.

CONTENTS

INTRODUCTION

These meditations were never meant to find their way into the
starkness of published print. They were written, in a longer
form, as scripts for broadcast and they were often tied to a
special time or season or an experience I had had which
illustrated something I felt was worth sharing at the time.
Almost all have in their broadcast form been transmitted on
Radio 4's "Lighten our Darkness" programmes which go out
on Saturday evenings at 11 pm. Studio 4 in Edinburgh looks
out through triple glazing over Queen Street in the centre of
the city to a private park on the other side of the road. Queen
Street is part of the Great North Road—the A1. But at night
an unreal quietness takes over from the busyness of the day
and with the studio lights dim and just two or, at most, three
colleagues and friends smiling through the glass from the
control cubicle it is quite easy to create an atmosphere in
words. The printed page is not like that. It has no rhythm of
itself. It is limited in shape or form − there are, after all, only
twenty-six different letter shapes. This is why I write in short
lines so that as I read my words into the microphone the
rhythm becomes a natural part of the phrasing. It is for this
reason that I never contemplated publishing these
meditations. They were experiential, they were my subjective
thoughts and images and, most of all, they were for speaking.

Then a number of people wrote to ask for a book of my
writings. I hadn't one to offer. Perhaps it would be right at
least to gather some of the scripts I had written and put them
into a shape for a book. This is the second attempt. If the
written word here is of help or comfort or if it offers some

new thoughts, then all the preparation will have been of value. The main purpose of my writing is to remind myself of the living God and his place in my life. If you can share that reminder and experience the love and comfort of God, the purpose is fulfilled.

I make just two suggestions. When these meditations were broadcast they were punctuated with music. Sometimes it was the majesty of the metrical psalms, sometimes the bare simplicity of a folk ballad. But mostly it was mood music from a number of sources, classical and modern. Music like Fauré's "Pavane" or Pachelbel's "Canon in D"; Sibelius' "Finlandia" and Mendelssohn's "Hebridean Overture"; and in more modern style, Erik Satie's "Gymnopodie No. 1" played by Sky and their "Carrillon"; "Dear Father" from Neil Diamond's "Jonathan Livingston Seagull" and "Aria" by Acker Bilk. And, of course, there are so many more, both classical and modern. Perhaps to play your favourite mood music would help the words of the meditations find their place. And the other suggestion is similar. The meditations were written for speaking. It may be that they would make their point best if, as you read them, you speak them silently or aloud and let them have again their rhythm.

Douglas Aitken

Dunfermline
July 1981

NEW

A new year is born
in a circus of celebration
toasts and toasties,
laughter and liquor,
loud promises of good behaviour
lasting a day at least
give or take an hour or two.
And then – reality:
the morning after;
the first few streaks of grey
across the darkened sky
proclaim the landmark past and duty calls.
Look out and measure that reality –
promises of poverty,
hardship and unemployment;
depression of state and soul;
pride, power and prejudice,
violence and hate;
imagined dignity stood on daily,
officiousness and self-importance,
corruption and intrigue;
groups of evil men infiltrating industry
bent on disruption and destruction;
strikes and work-to-rule;
bone-idleness and bitterness,
resentment and reprisal;
hunger, cold and insufficient shelter;
these are the harsh realities
that darken each new day,

the shadows on our destiny,
the cloud above our being.

Remember then
the sun still shines
from the fresh bright blueness
far above the cloud.
Remember then
the greyness of the dawn and morning frost
give way to streaks of gold and gentle warmth.
Remember then
the barren trees in winter
will turn to summer green
and drab and lifeless gardens
will blaze again so soon
in multicoloured life.
Remember then
and mark forever in the mind
the buds of love,
unworthy of the headlines,
the tiny acts of kindness,
the secret signs of care;
mere pinpoints of peace
that in due time
will burst the balloon of pride or hate
that disrupts us and divides
as surely as the flowers will bloom again
or skies be blue.

Look and see
amid the darkness of reality
the lights of life;
people who care and serve
and remember then
the Lord

the ultimate
the absolute
the source,
God
lives, rules and commands.

Jesus said:
This, then, is my commandment —
Love one another.

Lord,
Help us to love.

The possibility of prosperity
both temporal and eternal
lies in love alone.
Help us to love.

The dawn is drawing near.
Our dawn is overcast and grey
with hate and with division
and laziness
and selfishness
and violence
and pride.
Only love can clear the cloud.
Help us to love.

The new day is only hours away
and frost still sparkles on the ground.
The frost of our day
is racism —
black and white,
Jew and Arab,
cruelty, tyranny and power,

icicles of religious bigotry.
Only love can melt the frost.
Help us to love.

Across our world the same day breaks;
for some with cold,
for some with heat.
The sun we seek to warm our winter cold
is burning out the lives of others.
Their new dawn is distended bellies,
diseased eyes,
despairing hearts.
Only love can offer hope.
Help us to love.

As the first lightening of the sky
far in the east
declares another day
for us to face reality,
the enormity of the ill
with which our world abounds
is crystal clear;
and we are so weak, so small,
so very ineffectual
against so great a task.

But so is the tiny seed
beneath the hardened earth
that soon will grow and bloom
with beauty and with strength.
And every day demands of us
both actions and decisions
which by themselves are small
but which will touch so many lives.
So if we make at every dawn

a new commitment to love,
however weak that love may be
it will surely grow
and join with all other love
into a mighty irresistible power
to overcome.
Therefore, Lord,
help us to love.

Lord,
with every new year,
and every new day
and every new hour
let your love loose
on those in special need:
the aged and the tired,
the anxious and distressed,
those in danger of the elements
or of the violence of men;
and those especially in our minds,
our loved ones
wherever they may be.
Let your love bring warmth and strength
in every need.
And help us all to love.

Love is patient and kind;
It is not jealous or conceited or proud;
Love is not ill-mannered or selfish or irritable;
Love does not keep a record of wrongs;
Love is not happy with evil
but is happy with the truth.
Love never gives up.
Its faith, hope and patience never fail.
Love is eternal.

WINTER

It is winter.
Cold and frost and drifts of snow,
Communications chaos,
Isolation,
Silence,
Pain.

Winter.

Wild winds and mighty waves,
Ice,
Fog,
Death.

Winter.

Fur gloves and coats,
Log fires and hypothermia,
Frozen milk,
Cracked bones,
Sickness,
Hunger,
Insufficient circulation.

Winter.

Trees bare, stark and black,
With trembling brittle fingers
Clawing leaden skies
In dying desperation.

Gone,
Forgotten,
The summer green,
The autumn amber,
Like unlit traffic lights,
Useless,
Hopeless,
No contribution to any welfare,
No shelter from the wind and rain.

Winter.

The trough, the valley
Of constant discontent,
Discomfort,
Dismay,
Despair.

Chill and biting wind
Cutting keenly and remorselessly,
Physically and metaphorically,
Through layer upon layer
Of our protection.
Mountains of muffling,
The harbinger of damp and misery,
Gritted teeth and gasping breath
And quickly numbing face.
Rich and poor,
Young and old,
Everyman,
All know
And feel
The keen cutting power
Of the winter wind:
Numb skin,

Rough skin,
Raw skin,
Tears.

Winter.

The winter of our lives is more than cold:
It's disappointment, pain and loss,
And children flying from the fold
And good advice;
It's words spoken without thought
But not forgiven;
Hopes never reached,
Ambitions unfulfilled;
And age that presses on
With unrelenting beat
That brings a fear of death
With work undone.

Our winter.

But even now,
As nature's winter grips its victim
In an icy hand,
The unlit traffic lights begin to glow
A living red,
As red-tipped buds begin to burst
On barren branches.
Traffic lights
With red for GO,
To start the new beginning
Of the eternal nature sequence:
Red bud,
Green leaf,
Amber tint.

Tiny spots of expectation,
Not yet more
But signs unmistakable
Of continuing renewal.
Tiny buds
Growing to new branches,
Flowers and leaves;
A mighty glory in prospect
And certain.

So as we face the winter of our lives
And try to melt our fear
And wrap our qualms in human hope
And hide behind our mask
Our 'let's pretend'
And artificial smile,
Remember nature's cycle
Stirring eternally
Despite the cold
Under the snow,
Through the ice.
Remember – and hope.

Remember that I have commanded you
To be determined and confident.
Don't be afraid or discouraged,
For I, the Lord your God, am with you
Wherever you go.

Come, then, my love,
My darling, come with me.
The winter is over; the rains have stopped;
In the countryside the flowers are in bloom;
This is the time for singing;
The song of doves is heard in the fields;

Figs are beginning to ripen;
The air is fragrant with blossoming vines.
Come, then, my love,
My darling, come with me.

Jesus said:
I will be with you always,
To the end of the age.

Lord,
In their simplicity
Men of history laid in your charge
Times, seasons, elements and harvests.
And they prospered.
Uncomplicate us
That behind the mysteries of science
That cloud our faith
We may see and believe
In your control.

As the winter cold
Gives way again
To the fresh new life of spring
Help us in our living
To find the cycle of your love
To lift us from all gloom
And fears that would destroy us;

Let every day
And every hour
Be our new spring with you.

Into your eternal care
We commit ourselves
And those we love

And those in need;
That the promise of your presence
May be real to us all
Through all our living
Here and hereafter.
Amen.

PEACE

Peace is what I leave with you;
It is my own peace that I give you.
I do not give it as the world does.
Do not be worried and upset;
Do not be afraid.

Peace.

Strange how this mystery
so desired and so desirable,
even in the world's terms,
is so elusive.

Somehow we seem surrounded
by dispeace;
by tension, pressure, noise,
unrelenting noise,
traffic-rushing noise,
demolition and construction noise,
argument and bargain noise,
speed noise,
pressure noise,
factory noise,
pleasure noise,
deafening decibels of human endeavour,
human greed,
human pleasure;
always it is there
thundering in the ears,

crashing on the mind,
tiring the brain,
straining the heart.

Even in the quiet of the home
there is the family noise,
the bringing-up-of-children noise,
the facing-of-the-bills noise,
the coping-with-relationships noise.

Peace.

Shimmering in the heat of life,
mirage-like,
reached for, to disappear
in the act of reaching.

So we take time off;
climb into the hills;
fish lochs and rivers;
sit by the sea;
stroll through silent forest glades;
unwind;
recreate the body and the mind
by leaving all the stress behind
in search for sun
and silence.

How peaceful it is.

The tinkling of the burn,
the music of the shore,
the long, refreshing, sigh
of the wind in the trees;
the unhindered breeze

on the skin and through the hair
out there on the hill-tops.

How peaceful.

Until, of course,
the time is come to leave behind
the green and pleasant land,
the soft moss-covered forest track,
the shingle and the mountain path;
and tread once more the tarmac
and the paving slab,
playing life and death in traffic
facing again the pressures of living
and making a living.

The world's peace is real enough
but fleeting;
a passing respite
from the roar of life.

But Jesus said:
My peace I leave with you,
not the world's peace.
Mine.
Real, lasting, vital peace.

For disciples facing death
and persecution
not just then but in every age,
it has proved a powerful peace;
a deep contentment that they were not alone;
a hand in theirs
in time of trouble;
a whisper in the ear

like the whisper of the trees
silencing the noise of battle
and of stress;
a lightening of the vision
like the soul-refreshing view
from hill-top and from cliff,
banishing all strain.

His peace,
that hope-releasing faith
which captivates the heart and mind
in the middle of life,
in the noise of living.

His peace
which is always there
wherever we may go.

His peace,
always.

Lord,
Let your peace possess us now.
Calm our troubled minds
every new day.
Release the burden
of the things we have not done
which ought to have been done;
and the things we have done
which ought not to have been done;
of the things done badly,
the things done hastily
and the things done too slowly.

Give us a new space in our lives,

space to be ourselves
as you created us to be.

Let your peace
save us from human pressure,
lift us from human despair,
recreate us
new every morning,
still us to rest
new every night;

That in all things we may know
and be
and share
peace.

The peace of God
which passes human understanding
keep us all
tonight,
tomorrow
and for ever.
Amen.

DEATH

Death is destroyed; victory is complete.
Where, Death, is your victory?
Where, Death, is your power to hurt?
Death gets its power to hurt from sin,
and sin gets its power from the Law.
But thanks be to God who gives us the victory
through our Lord Jesus Christ.

Strange, isn't it,
in the middle of living
to talk about death?

But often enough
that's how it happens –
suddenly,
awfully,
in the middle of life,
death.

But then, why not?
For if there is one thing in life that's certain,
for sure,
in absolute terms,
it's that one day,
some time,
we'll die.
Some day,
in the twinkling of an eye,
all the restlessness,

17

the noise,
the pressure,
the anxieties and the fears,
the sorrows and the joys of this world
will be over,
done,
behind us.

Now, most of us would be glad
to get rid of all those things
but the last thing we want to talk about
is death;
and we don't want to talk about it
because it is a door
into the unknown;
a mystery;
and as far as we can tell
our experience in this world
comes to an end.

And that isn't always convenient.
There are bills unpaid,
arrangements unmade,
engagements unfulfilled,
children to be educated,
grandchildren to be spoiled,
a million things to do.

No, death is not convenient;
so let's put it off
because it is an end,
a conclusion,
a finality.

But is it?
Here's what St. Paul believed:

Our brothers, we want you to know
the truth about those who have died,
so that you will not be sad
as are those who have no hope.
We believe that Jesus died and rose again
and so we believe that God will take back with Jesus
those who have died believing in him.

Death is just a part of life,
not an end,
just a stage.

The Psalmist, too, was sure
in Psalm 23,
the Shepherd Psalm.
The verse about death
is in the middle
not at the end;
not this world,
then the next
but life on both sides.
And that is good.

The fact that death is just a part of life
and not the end
means that this life can be enjoyed,
filled with vitality
and creativity
and humour
and life,
because every day
this side and the other of death

is an adventure,
a gift from God.

And if your journey in this life
is tortured by pain
or sickness or sadness,
let the hope
and the certainty
of a new world to come
when in God's time it comes for you,
let that hope
be at least a light
to lighten your darkness
a little.

Lord,
It is very easy to be afraid of death.
When we are young there is too much to do;
In middle age
our responsibilities are too great;
As we grow old
it comes too near.

Help us to find in your word
both comfort and conviction;
release us from our fear
to make the most of life
both sides of eternity.

Into your safe-keeping we commend
all who are on the brink of death,
especially those who have waited
with impatience or in pain
or frustration at infirmity

and those who in human terms
are far too young to die.

And we ask for your comfort
for those who wait with the dying
that they too may find
the certainty of eternity.

Lord,
for ourselves
we simply ask
peace and expectation
when it is our turn
to pass through the door of death
into eternal life
with you.
Amen.

CONVICTION

I am certain that nothing can separate us
from the Love of God;
neither death nor life,
neither angels nor other heavenly rulers or powers,
neither the present nor the future,
neither the world above nor the world below;
there is nothing in all creation
that will ever be able to separate us
from the love of God
which is ours through Christ Jesus our Lord.

Conviction.

The certainty that the hoped-for
is reality itself.
Of course we have convictions.
We change them every day:
opinions about people
or politics or science;
convictions about policy
economy or commerce;
our views,
quite often strongly held,
but always open wide to change.
Convictions,
convenient branches on which to pause
as, squirrel-like, we leap
from tree to tree
or hope to hope.

It has to be so.
If it were not so,
if scientists or engineers
did not cling to convictions
until they're proved untrue,
there never would be progress;
for once a theory's stated
and held as being right
the challenge is to prove it wrong
and take another step
along the way of understanding.
Convictions are just staging posts
or stepping stones
along our human way;
they stimulate enthusiasm
and give us stable ground
on which to build.
But the very openness to change
which our convictions have
and must have of necessity
makes us very vulnerable
subject to doubt
and fear
and indecision
and mental disarray.
It makes us war-like and possessive
lest anyone should take from us
by proof or implication
our conviction.

Our need above all need
is one solid ground
which will not move
which does not change

even if the world would end
or men be good.

St. Paul has that conviction
about the love of God.
He says:
Nothing in the whole world,
not measurement
not life
not even death
not the powers of men
not his right or wrong
not the power of evil
not the power of good
not the present
not anything that the future may hold
nothing
can change
break
destroy
or take away
God's love for his creation:
Us.

Now, that is some conviction.

It also means
if death cannot destroy
the love of God
that love is there
in the hereafter too.
And that means
that the love of God is the strength
by which we cope with this life
and the next as well.

Or put another way:
there is no experience of life
where God is not present,
not even death.

Jesus said:
I go to prepare a place for you.

That means God cares and loves
now and forever.
Grasp that conviction
and live.

Father,
Convince us of your love.

We place ourselves very firmly into your care
for life or death
and life tomorrow
here or hereafter,
so that wherever tomorrow may find us
we may live it with vitality
and conviction.

Then, we place our loved ones and our friends
acquaintances and colleagues
from office, shop, club or factory,
fellow queuers at the bus-stop,
all of them, into your care
that they may find
if they don't already know it
the comfort and the conviction
of you beside us all through life.

And, finally, we place our world

with all its chaos and its pain,
its terror and its shame,
its tyranny and hate,
its hunger and its cold,
its sadness and its loneliness,
we place our world
into your care
that same care
that never ends
so that through the darkness
the light of your dawn may shine
and our world may find
conviction in your love.

These things we ask
through Jesus Christ
our Lord.
Amen.

LONELINESS

As the darkness of evening
draws its velvet coat around the day,
it is a time to feel alone,
to know the cool of loneliness.

Of course, there are degrees
and kinds of loneliness,
real and imagined,
and self-inflicted,
like the loneliness of the long-distance runner
or the solo-yachtsman;
the loneliness of the personal fight
for victory over ill-health.
Or there's the loneliness
of the searcher after solitude,
walking in the hills
or gliding on thermals
high above the world,
looking for peace and quiet
to regenerate the body,
the spirit and the mind.
And there's the loneliness
of end-of-tether tiredness,
of end-of-work-week weariness.
And that's a kind of loneliness
that all of us must know.

Lord,
we come at the end of this day

27

tired by its activity,
wearied by its worry,
ashamed of its memories;
we come
simply to find companionship.

Make us, now,
as aware of your presence with us
as we are of being ourselves,
that in that presence
we may find your peace.

Be still, my soul: the Lord is on thy side;
Bear patiently the cross of grief or pain;
Leave to thy God to order and provide;
In every change he faithful will remain.
Be still, my soul: thy best, thy heavenly Friend
Through thorny ways leads to a joyful end.

Note those great words:
Leave to thy God
to order and provide;
In every change
he faithful will remain.

That, of course,
is as it should be:
God, the constant
in a changing world;
God, the controller and provider
for the loneliness
of each individual thorny road
to the future.

The trouble is that we are human
and even when we do believe
we often wonder if that faith
is sure or sane.
For we are quickly moved
to wonder and to tears
by great and rousing words
and by majestic music
to which we sing them;
and in these moving moments
find God a little nearer.

But the real need of our being
is much deeper,
much more lasting that can be met
by a moment of magnificent music;
the need of our being is to be free
from the burden of loneliness
that eats away our selfhood
and breeds fear and despair.

Be still, my soul: thy God doth undertake
To guide the future as he has the past.
Thy hope, thy confidence let nothing shake;
All, now mysterious, shall be bright at last.
Be still, my soul: the waves and wind still know
His voice who ruled them while he dwelt below.

It is to make the assurance of those words
a physical reality
for body and for spirit
that is the root of our need.

Of course, there is the real
physical loneliness of those

whose circumstances have left them alone,
uncared-for, unremembered;
noticed only by neighbours
as that old hermit,
that blot on the district,
or by the milkman on his rounds;
and then unnoticed in their absence,
until the headlines claim
their lonely tragic death.

For that kind of loneliness
there's no excuse.
True, we wish our privacy to be respected.
But it is not privacy to die alone.
We *are* neighbours to our neighbours,
we *are* our brothers' keepers,
for our society's sake
if not for God's.

Nor is it privacy
to reject the neighbours' friendship
because at the time it comes
things are going well.
The cure of loneliness is love
and love needs two
to be complete:
one to give,
one to receive, to accept,
to respond, in turn, with love
and so complete the circle of love.
No. There's no excuse
for physical loneliness;
not really.

Of course, there's always the loneliness

of memory of past joys,
of rooms once filled with light and noise
now dim and sadly quiet;
but the loneliness of memory
can bring meaning and value
to the evening of life
as long as someone cares
sometimes . . .

Lord,
we know you care
for all your creation.
Help us to care
with your kind of care
for those around us
that their loneliness
and ours
may give way to peace.
Amen.

BEING ALONE

Alone.

It is a feeling filled with fear,
with awesome apprehension,
like standing in the centre of a city
surrounded by the bustle of life,
the streets all flooded with its folk
on way to work or shop or home,
and know no word
no person
no place or haven.
In all the fears of life
that kind of being alone
can chill the spine.
Yet all around you
fellow-strangers walk
divided from the city
and from you
by language, race or purpose
and like yourself
suffering the agony of being alone
within a crowd.

Nor does it need a foreign place
to feel alone
for it can happen here
even in the family group.

It is the aloneness of the platform

or the pulpit
or the classroom
or the office;
it can be an oppressive aloneness
destroying self
even among friends
even praying friends.
And worse,
there is the feeling of not being understood
even by those you know
who love you with a passionate love;
children growing up,
developing, experimenting
among parents out of their depth;
parents watching with apprehension
those same children
growing and departing.

The aloneness of not being trusted
or confided in.

The aloneness of standing out
against the norm,
the odd one out
at the party
or the assembly
or the meeting
among the friends
you thought you knew.

That kind of being alone
is hard to bear
but it is real.
And no-one escapes completely.

But God said to Joshua
in his greatest time of being alone
when he became the leader
of the people of Israel,
God said:

Be determined and confident!
Don't be afraid or discouraged,
for I, the Lord your God am with you
wherever you go.

And Jesus said to the disciples
at their moment of feeling alone
even beside each other
when he was about to depart from their sight,
Jesus said:

I will be with you always,
to the end of the age.

It is the ability to grasp that,
that the Love of God is real,
that the presence of God is fact,
that the promises of God are kept;
it is the ability to grasp that
which is the source of comfort
in that special kind of being alone
which all of us must sometimes share.

First, there is the human assurance
that we are not alone
in our feelings of aloneness,
for we share a common frailty
whatever face we put upon it.

Then there is the openness to God's help
which acceptance and awareness
of our inadequacy provide.

And, finally,
like Christ in the total aloneness
of the garden of Gethsemane,
there is the full commitment
of all our life to God.

Father, your will be done.

Our strength and comfort
begins and ends
in God.

Lord,
Comfort our feelings of being alone.
Calm our fearfulness.
Stand beside us through the darkness.
Walk before us through the day.
Help us to hope for
and work for the hope of
your peace in our future
and the future of our children
because you, alone, are Lord.

Into your hands, Lord,
we give this night
the history of our world,
the pain of all mankind,
the potential of humanity
and the honest work of hands.

Into your care, Lord,

we commit all people,
especially those in danger
or in special kind of need;
and we commit ourselves
and all we love
that your will be done
in them and us
to your glory
and our eternal peace.

And the peace of God
which passes understanding
be with us all
for evermore.
Amen.

LETHARGY

Sometimes
in the middle of the winter
when everything is cold and wet
the sun comes out
in an advertising campaign
for spring.
Of course there's still some winter
yet to come;
of course the rain is never far behind,
nor until after Easter
is snow to be forgotten.
But those short sun-brightened days
of winter
are a comfort and a promise
of seasons yet to come;
they call to mind those blissful times before us
when there will be no need to rush
or rise up with the dawn to work
but only time to rest and laze
and let the lethargy of life
take full command.

And so it does.
Nor just in times of rest
and recreation.
So often in our lives
the thought of effort
is too much;
the very act of rising

far too great;
and lethargy the best way out,
its evil side
biting at the very roots
of our efficiency and work.

How difficult it is
when things pile up
to bring ourselves to face them;
to lift a hand to help,
a thought to share;
how difficult to smile
or show a sign of hope
when all the future seems so black
and void of life;
how difficult to have a faith
when all that's wrong before our eyes
can find success,
while all that's good must work so hard
to prove itself.
How easy then to let things go
and just give up,
to cease the care and tidiness
that marked our work
and all our lives
and let the evil side of lethargy
take full command.
It waits to do just that.

When the dear light of one you love
is taken from your side
and you are left alone
to cope;
or when the trust you thought you had
in those you serve

is cast away
and you are left
without a friend;
or when the job that promised you
security and peace
is suddenly and finally
reduced from years to days
and all the prospects it held out
have vanished in the dust
of some directive from afar
unhindered by concern;
or when the things you plan
with so much care
fall flat or fail;
or illness takes a toll
with unexpected force
when you are on the point of making good;
or children in their time
fall short of all your hopes
or even bring you shame
by standards you have set;
when your whole world,
with all its good and bad,
the ways that you have known
and set your future by,
when all of that decays
and crumbles in your sight,
temptation rises to give in
and lethargy stands by
to move its forces in.

It happens
with such awful ease
and soon one feels no pain,

but just a weakening weariness
devoid of any hope.

Our winter is like that
with February half done.
It seems so long to spring
and blossoms on the tree;
the stark bare branches reach out still
towards the leaden skies
and make no visual effort
to break out into bloom.
They take so long;
they laze,
lethargic in the winter's grip,
like hibernating animals
unwilling to come out
and face another year
of foraging for food.

So slender blinks of sunshine
amid the winter frost
are soft and warm reminders
of future hope.

Lord,
In the winter of our lives
when the energy of will
gives way to lethargy and doubt,
be the ray of winter sun
which holds a golden promise
of faith and hope and love;

Surround us with the comfort
and the counsel that we need
for all the human problems

that each of us will meet
and keep us in the faith
that you are ever there
in every situation, in which
we find ourselves enmeshed.

So, even in the fiercest fight
we have to make our way;
we know your very presence
will stand forever
by our side.

Into your loving hands
we offer for your care
all those who find this night
the darkness of the sky
is spreading to their life,
that you may be their comfort
their soul-reviving light
and we may be your servants
in helping them to live.

Warm us, Lord
to be your sun of love
in the winter of our days
that lethargy may have no ground
to build its soul-destroying power.

So may our days shine with your light.
Amen.

ENERGY

*I have the strength to face all conditions
by the power that Christ gives me.*

Energy in human terms
just bubbles over
like the tireless tumble-tension
of children growing up,
expressed in endless motion
from dawn till after dusk;
there is the adult passion
for hobby or for work
consuming every hour of time
and every spark of love;
there is the full commitment
to church or club or cause
that takes first place
in goods and time
before all other things;
there is the family circle
demanding so much time
yet often left neglected
while energies are spent elsewhere.

It is the price of life
to face the fact of energy,
of human effort stored within
the body, mind or soul
just waiting for release.
It is the pain of life

to channel that potential
into a thousand places
which need the power in store.
The wisdom how to do that
is rarely easily found,
nor is it always what we would choose
or find to be convenient
or suitable to our desire
or preference or whim.

So, energy that is to hand
is often wasted,
squandered on our pride,
as energy from sun and wind
around us every day
is cast aside
unharnessed and unhindered.
For even some few feeble rays
of a winter sun,
hidden, perhaps, by snow-filled clouds,
could warm, at least,
a city's water heating;
as the strong winds
that whistle from the west,
from dark Atlantic waters
and icy Arctic wastes
across our winter scene
could turn, on almost any day
a windmill pump
or power source.
But all this energy goes to waste
as we press on with other schemes
more scientific and more tangible
than the pale yellow of the sun
and the soft whisper of the wind.

Yet they are there,
the gift of God,
like every other source of power.

So we,
in human lives,
can waste so much of value.
The energy of bodies
cast aside by unemployment,
by unwillingness to invest;
the energy of growing minds
turned to evil plans
or waste,
because a parent doesn't care,
encourage or support,
or says to go to higher schools
is waste of earning time;
the energy of human spirits
denied the freedom they require
to grow and make a better world
because it's feeble to have faith,
or inconvenient to believe
in a God of love,
when power and wealth
are what the world regards
as signs of true success.

Such waste
is inexcusable
but real.
For all its possibility,
our energy
can draw us down.
Until,
that is,

we bring to mind
the promises of God,
the freedom that his Word sets out,
the love that is the key.

*I have the strength to face all conditions
by the power that Christ gives me.*

Lord,
we offer you our energy
of body, mind and soul,
to use in us as you desire
according to your will.
We offer you our children
that, in your blessing them,
you may release for future years
their energy, controlled
by your more perfect plan.
We offer you our elders
towards the evening of their lives
for you to comfort and to bless,
encourage and sustain;
that where they've tried to give themselves,
their energy and power,
to do your will
and live your way
your commendation may be clear;
and where they've failed
or fallen short
your mercy will fill in;
we offer you ourselves
whatever be our years
that we may from this evening hour
be kept in paths of right,
our last remaining energy

directed by your law,
to give and serve,
in word and act,
until the time
you call us home.

Lord,
this world of yours,
which we have so destroyed,
has spent the energy of men
in self-destruction and dispeace,
in power-seeking wars,
in self-aggrandisement and hate;
this world of yours
needs new direction, new control.
Begin in us
your transformation,
that we may share
the way of love
which is your key
to everlasting peace.

For Jesus' sake,
Amen.

LITTLE THINGS

Strange, isn't it,
how the first hint of frost
can change even clear blue skies
from sign of summer
into certainties of winter
and send us to the cupboard
to rescue jerseys
and switch on central heating
or light the first of winter's fires
and give the grass its final cut
until next spring.

Strange, isn't it,
how quickly autumn tints begin to show
and how the picture starts to change
from verdant greens to russet red
and browns and gold,
new colour codes
begun by frost,
a mere suggestion that the time has come
to don the winter's barren garb
and all at once it comes:
so little to begin so much.

It's always that in life itself:
a letter with a single line
can darken a day,
destroy a hope,
transform a life;

47

a single inch
can measure out from life to death;
a tiny shift of rock
far down within the earth
can cause a shape of beauty to appear
or wreck ten thousand human lives,
or both;
a single flicker of the eye
can change the safety of a car
into a crushing case of death.
An inch, a foot,
a second, a moment,
too far, too long,
the world becomes a different place
and we become transformed and changed
for good or ill,
for joy or sorrow,
for riches or poverty,
different.
So little to begin so much.

Of course, the real dramatic things
which change the lives of men
in the briefest space of time
always happen to the other one,
and not to us;
the fire is always down the street,
the accident across the road;
the letter with the tragic news
falls through the other letter-box;
the neighbour is the one in jail,
the cripple comes from over there;
it's always someone else
to whom disasters happen
and not to us.

But, of course, they do;
we know they do,
not all of them,
not all at once,
but some of them to all of us;
there's no escape from sadness
and some have more than others;
there's no escape from pain
and some have worse than others;
there's no escape from worry,
like caring for a child
who's just left home
or stays out too late
and some have greater cause than others;
there's no escape from love
and some love hurts more than others;
there's no escape from death
and some death is more tragic than others;
and all these things
and many more
are, at the time,
the greatest and the harshest thing
that comes to us,
but in the span of life
that is this world
they are so small.

Little things have great results
like the widening circles on a glass-still loch
from the settling of an insect
or the falling of a leaf,
in time to tinkle on the shore,
a tiny wave.

But if the little things that reach us most

are tragedy and sorrow
and nothing more
we miss the most important thing:
the power of little acts of good.
Of course, the headlines only show
the mighty deeds of human good,
the rescue from a blazing ship
or from a narrow mountain ledge,
the life that's lost to save a child;
and so they should.

But that is not the end of good;
it's just the best of all writ large.
The smallest act of kindness
by the simplest, shyest one of us
is less demanding and dramatic
but, like the widow's mite,
is just as fruitful in its work.

Lord,
Keep us mindful of the little things
that all of us can do
to make the world a richer place
in friendship and community.
Help us to see beyond
the simplicity of kindness
to the power of self-giving love
that gives it strength.
Make us aware that just a word
or act of simple courtesy
is not to be simplistic
or naive
but to do your holy will.

Open our eyes and ears

to your word of counsel
in all our dealings with our fellow-men
that we may have patience
and understanding
and compassion
and most of all
your kind of love.

Lord,
make us aware of the frailty of human life
and the strength of your lasting love
that in that strength
we may live the knife-edge of humanity
in confidence and peace
till death shall take us
from the little things of this world
to eternity and infinity
with you.
Amen.

COURAGE

How often have you been brave today
or through this week?

Of course,
there are many kinds of bravery,
for courage is a quality
that makes demands
at many levels of our living,
and on all of us.

It takes a kind of courage
to drive a train
or go down a mine
or dive deep in the ocean;
it takes courage to go on patrol
round an Ulster street,
or test-fly a plane,
or try a new drug;
it takes courage to do a thousand things
both great and small
and it matters not
how often you do them,
it always takes courage.

Without the constant courage
of countless ordinary folk,
facing raging seas,
or dark passages beneath the earth,
keeping long and lonely vigils through the night

or speeding with the pace of sound
across the skies,
without them and their courage
we could not live.

Now, that is worth a thought.

Lord,
we thank you for ordinary people
whose ordinary jobs
make extraordinary demands upon them:
for divers and miners,
firemen and pilots,
fishermen and police,
merchantmen and nurses,
members of the armed forces
and all the countless others
who, even now,
overcome their fears with busyness
to serve us and our freedom.
We ask your courage, Lord,
that they may work in safety
and we,
having remembered them,
may rest in peace.
Amen.

But courage is not limited
to the facing of physical danger.
Without doubt,
as these words are read
and thought about,
there are those whose very breathing
demands courage:
those who are never free

from pain,
or handicap,
or disability.

To face this unsympathetic world
without complaint
is courage of a special order.
How often does a minister or priest
call upon a pain-wracked parishioner
to offer solace from the Spirit
and come away refreshed himself
with the same courage
comfort and strength
he went there to give.

That sort of courage
is born of faith,
a total faith.
It is a faith that expects results.

The Psalmist had that kind of faith,
the faith that expects results,
the faith that covered
every experience of life
with confidence and assurance
because without it
there is nothing
and with it, everything.

The Lord is my shepherd;
I have everything I need.
He lets me rest in fields of green grass
and leads me to quiet pools of fresh water.
He gives me new strength.

He guides me in the right paths,
as he has promised.
Even if I go through the deepest darkness,
I will not be afraid, Lord,
for you are with me.
Your shepherd's rod and staff protect me.

You prepare a banquet for me,
where all my enemies can see me;
you welcome me as an honoured guest
and fill my cup to the brim.
I know that your goodness and love
will be with me all my life;
and your house will be my home
as long as I live.

In that kind of assurance
all courage is possible;
without it
even life itself
becomes a mountain of fears
and pains
with only human hands
to help the climb.

Lord,
we commend to your care
those whose suffering demands courage;
let their faith
and your presence
be sufficient for them.

We think of those
who struggle through this life
facing its problems and its pains

in their own strength
and the human help
of friends.
Reach out with your touch of healing
for body, mind and spirit,
and let our trust
show out the brightness of your love
that they may believe
and find their faith
and the courage for living
that only you can give.

Lighten the darkness, Lord
of every life
surrounded by sorrow
or pain
or anxiety
or shame
or anger
or hate,
that in your lightening
they
and we
may find your peace.
Amen.

DECISIONS

Jesus said:

In the world
You are going to have trouble.
But courage!
I have conquered the world.

The trouble with living
is that all day
and every day
we have to make decisions.

Some of them are very small
like whether to go out
or not
or what to read
or write
or make;
and some of them are very great;
how we shall live
and make or break our family;
shall honesty and truth
be hallmarks of our way
or not;
one way or the other
we must decide.

And often our decision
affects the lives of others

just as the ripple
from a pebble popped in a pool
will in good time
disturb the shore
all round the pool.

It might be a decision
to terminate a job
and send to unemployment
some loyal family man;
it might be a decision
when terrorists abound
to rescue some poor hostage
by force of arms
and put at risk
the hostage and his captor
and those who must go in.

It might be almost anything
on which we must decide
but we must still be mindful
of all it will affect
and search our reason
and the motive
which makes us choose
the way we choose
and not a different way.

In all our life's decisions
both great and small
we must be sure
that they are right
and will not lie
upon our lives for ever

in regret.
But that is never easy.

Maybe the decision
is a matter of our conscience
that calls for action;
but that action will affect security
or pride or aspirations
or even our future;

Maybe it's a determination to succeed
at any cost
that leads us to accept the unacceptable
because the fear of failure
fills the mind;

Maybe it's sincere compassion
that hides the reality
that some hurtful word or action,
quickly said or done,
with love,
is more compassionate.

But such decisions
and hundreds like them
are ours to make today,
tomorrow,
next week,
and all our life.
And as long as we nurse our fears about them
so long will our wisdom fail
and truth and justice,
right and love
will be for ever lost.

So Jesus says to us,
Look, it's often hard
and will go on being so;
but set your mind at rest
I have defeated the world.

Christ promises to help us
in the life that he has given us
and that's a promise
that is never broken;
in all the uncertainty of the world
that, at least, is sure.

So, as this day
sighs to a close,
put your trust in that promise
and make the right decisions for living
with confidence.

Lord,
in all the things that trouble us,
the work we have to do,
the decisions we have to make,
the words we have to say,
the actions we have to take,
be the source of our wisdom
the strength of our decisiveness
and the pillar of our peace.

Lord,
we commend to your care
those whose decisions
determine the destiny of mankind:
presidents and ministers,
generals and industrialists,

spies and civil servants;
be the conscience that restrains,
the wisdom that constructs
and the power that saves
from dangerous wrong.

Lord,
into your hands
we place those we love
and ourselves;
that, in the certainty of your promises,
we may find today
and forever
the power to be.
Amen.

LIGHT

Midsummer, plus a week.
The longest day was past.
Already the nights were drawing in.
Already the long night-streaks of light
were less.
Already the darkness of winter
had begun its slow journey,
imperceptibly at first,
to envelop us.
And all too soon
the days would pass unnoticed,
beginning after we start at work,
ending before us,
leaving us travelling
in perpetual darkness.

So there was contrast
on a journey, north, to Orkney,
stopping on midsummer's night
across the bridge at Bonar Bridge,
to look south
from a favourite hotel
late into the night
over the still waters
of the Dornoch Firth
to the silent hills of Struie;
the stillness broken
only by the rising trout

and paddling swan
living in perpetual day.

Then, on by boat from Scrabster
across the Pentland Firth
shimmering in sparkling sunlight,
rising and falling gently
in the Atlantic and the North Sea swell,
past the bright-red sandstone stack,
the rugged challenge to mountaineers,
the Old Man of Hoy,
to disembark at Stromness
and journey on by road to Kirkwall
where, in the middle of the year,
the darkness never wins its will
against the midnight light.
And in these longest days
there lies eternal hope.

Hope,
says St. Paul,
is a certainty
where God is concerned.
And, in the lingering dusk
meeting the early dawn half-way,
cutting out the night,
there is the certainty
that darkness is not for ever;
that the great and little darknesses
that shade our human lives from time to time
and seem eternal
will give way to light;
that the deepest shadow
of death and sorrow
has a new dawn and lasting light beyond it;

that there will be
in the future, as in the past,
long summer nights of life
where there is no darkness at all.

The vision of St. John,
in the Book of Revelation,
of the New Jerusalem,
the eternity to which we are called,
is a vision of a world
where there is no more darkness,
nor tears,
nor pain.

Midsummer in the Northern Isles
is a promise of that even now.

Lord,
in the world around us
we see your promises
renewed every day;
in day that follows night,
in sunshine after rain,
in summer after winter.
And still we find it hard
fully to believe.
Give us faith, Lord,
and forgive our unbelief.

Our darkness is the sorrow
that shadows every life;
the greed and pride and power
that make us hard to like;

Our darkness is the weakness
in body and in mind,
that makes us less than able
to make our mark or take our place
among our fellow men;

Our darkness is the loneliness
so many people feel,
unwanted and uncared-for
in the evening of their day;

Our darkness is the shade of death
upon our earthly life,
our apprehension and our fear
of what might lie ahead;

Our darkness is our pain,
our helplessness and age,
the weariness with work and life
that saps our very will;

Our darkness is to realise
that all we've sought to do
and give ourselves in service to
is not enough,
or good enough,
or wrong;
that we have lost
or never had
the trust of those we serve;

Our darkness is the inner ill
we bring upon ourselves

by trusting in our human strength
to do your holy will.

Lord,
by the lasting light
of the midnight sun,
restore to us the certainty
our darkness will not last;
that it will make way for lightness,
for brightness and for hope;
that in the very deepest trough
we find ourselves today
you will,
as you have promised, Lord,
lighten our darkness
and surround us with your love.
Amen.

CALM

Jesus stood up
and commanded the wind,
Be quiet!
and he said to the waves,
Be still!
The wind died down
and there was a great calm.
Then Jesus said to his disciples,
Why are you frightened?
Have you still no faith?

One of the most dangerous waters
around our shores
is the Pentland Firth,
where the North Sea and Atlantic
vie for victory
against each other,
dashing their mighty rollers
into each other,
commanding their powerful winds
to churn the millpond
into a maelstrom,
trapping even sturdy ships
and sea-wise sailors
in their icy grip
and thrusting them
with frightening ease
against the rugged cliffs
of Orkney,

67

while the brave men of Hoy
at Longhope
and all the other lifeboat crews
risk life and limb to save them.

The gently northward-dipping ferry
Saint Ola
and the white-topped azure of the Firth
on other days
are promise still
of saving calm
that follows all the storms of life.

This is no sentimental myth,
for in the Pentland storms
good men have died
to save their fellows;
and sacrifice is never wholly void,
nor is their sacrifice unlike
the sacrifice of Christ.

And after every storm
there is a calm
a respite,
a refuge and a peace.

Along the eastern coast of Orkney
hard up on to the rocks
beneath the towering cliffs
there stands a wreck,
a merchant ship
rusty and rotten
discarded by the sea,
a monument to the frailty of men
against the mighty sea.

The crew were saved by Breeches buoy
and lived to sail again;
but in the rescue in the Firth
the Longhope men put out to sea
and never came back.
Next day the volunteers
to take their absent place
outnumbered those who'd left
and died,
who had to be replaced.

It's that same self-denying love
a thousand times more pure
that Jesus pours into the world
to calm our storms
and rescue us
from fear and danger
grief and pain.

So was the calm that Jesus gave
on the fishing sea of Galilee
when the wind was still
and the waters calm
and the hearts of his disciples
in the time of their distress
found a new and lasting peace.

The Pentland calm
is certain hope,
assurance once again
that God is able still
and wills
to give us calm and peace.

And more than that

to do without our faith;
for after he had stilled the storm
he challenged all their trust;
he'd saved their lives
and brought order in
where fear and chaos reigned
while they had stood in terror
faithless in their fear.

How much more then,
will be the calm
in life and heart
when we believe?

Lord,
we live our lives
from storm to storm:
the anger and impatience
that marks our human frame;
the war-like words and actions,
the massing of our arms;
the careless casual treatment
of other nations' good.
Our storms are our anxiety
for children growing up
and turning into adults
before our very eyes,
our unwillingness to let them go
and be themselves.
Our storms are all the tensions
we raise between ourselves:
our prejudice and hatred,
intolerance and scorn;
the casting up of all the wrongs
we count and keep in store;

the unjust wrath and bitterness
we nurse to keep them warm –

These are the human storms
we bring upon our lives.

Lighten our darkness, Lord
calm our dispeace;
and in that calm of Christ
help us to find for ever
a new and living faith
in your eternal care.

And let your gracious blessing
come on those in special need
and rest upon our loved ones
wherever they may be;
and bring to all, your healing
in body, mind and soul
and strength for each tomorrow
and hope beyond our dreams
until, at last, we see you
forever face to face.
Amen.

TRANQUILLITY

Tranquillity
is what we all crave for
so much of the time
and what we miss
more than attain.

Even now
tranquillity escapes us
if we let our minds run back
over the day that's past;
or begin to think
about tomorrow.

Tranquillity,
so much desired,
so seldom gained,
because we will not stop
and let it possess us.

In the hills and in the forests
there is one kind of tranquillity.

It isn't in the beauty,
though beauty there is.
It is in the seugh,
the sighing of the wind in the trees,
the tinkling of a woodland stream,
the silence of the forest,
the soft spring of pine-needle-covered peat under foot,

the shafts of golden sun through the fingers of the firs,
tracing bright and bold patterns of light and shade
save in the deepest forest;
and there
where trees are tall and straight and dense,
to happen upon a red deer
and for a fleeting moment
meet eye to eye.

That is tranquillity.

In that same tranquillity
one day
on the morning boat
from Colonsay to Oban
we watched the dawn
stretch its golden fingers
across a leaden sky
in ever-changing patterns
of colour and intensity
until suddenly — too soon —
it was day again
and the tranquillity transformed
into the pressure of the morning,
leaving only its memory
to soothe the mind.

Lord,
we thank you
for every experience of tranquillity
in our fast-moving world
the magic of a breaking dawn,
the silence of the forest,
the roaring of a rushing stream,
the majesty of hills;

the sudden silence of a city street
between the traffic noise,   ———> (rural)
the emptiness of a Sunday road,
the calm of a country field
where the sound of bees
is deafening.

We thank you
for all our individual times of calm,
treasured seconds of respite
remembered
long after they are gone.

Give us, Lord,
wisdom to make the most
of each moment of tranquillity
and courage to carry its renewal
into our whole being.   AMEN.

But there is more:
under that magic dawn
breaking so beautifully
over the Island of Scarba,
there was the pounding roar
of the whirlpool of Corryvreckan
where all the mighty power
of the Atlantic swell,
seeking to reach the shore
of the long arm of Kintyre
right down to the Mull,
finds its way barred
by a whisper of islands:
Islay and Jura,
Colonsay and Scarba;
and rushes with a roaring rage

through the tiny gap
between Jura and Scarba,
the Gulf of Corryvreckan,
boiling the waters into a foaming whirl
where many a sailor
has sailed his last.

Under the tranquillity of the dawn,
the violence of the waves.

And that's where tranquillity
the real tranquillity
that lasts beyond the respite
must be found.

Not just in the holiday walk
nor in the Sunday stroll
but right in the middle
of the week,
in the middle of life
at its worst and at its toughest.

That's where God's tranquillity
is to be found
and for living
that's all we need.

Lord,
in our lives
there is trouble,
always trouble;
anxiety and temptation,
bitterness and pain,
pressure and weariness,
tragedy and sorrow.

Somehow
sometime
all of us come to the point
when everything is too much
and we cannot cope.

Lord,
let your tranquillity
fill our hearts,
free our souls
and complete our lives.
Amen.

FAITH

I believe in God
The Father Almighty,
Maker of Heaven and Earth;
And in Jesus Christ,
His only Son,
Our Lord.

So says the Creed;
And we believe
or say we do.
But do we mean what others mean?
Or is our claim to faith unique?

Isn't it a fact
that people's ideas about God
are as numerous as people themselves?
From the spirit that moves
through the jungle at night,
to the Mungu who dwells
in the snows of Kirinyaga;
or from the kind old man
with the long flowing beard,
to the mysterious, unapproachable
creator of all;
or from the God of wrath and war
in the fury of the elements,
to the loving gentle Jesus
meek and mild;
and a thousand other views

like the ultimate perfection,
the supreme mind,
the perfect word;
all of them, understandings
of him whom we call God.

No wonder it is difficult
to find a common mind on God.
Yet men do believe more deeply
than by the colour of the sky
or tiny children's fingers
and perfection of a flower;
men do believe beyond the sight
of things around the world.

Lord . . .
Where could I go to escape from you?
Where could I get away from your presence?
If I went up to heaven, you would be there;
If I lay down in the world of the dead,
You would be there;
If I flew away beyond the east,
Or lived in the farthest place in the west,
You would be there to lead me,
You would be there to help me.

For the Psalmist this was the key:
that God was inescapable;
his beginning and his end,
the source of life itself,
knowing him,
caring for him,
protecting him
from conception to the grave.
It is a belief

born from simplicity
that could be desirable
particularly in our time
when the conquests and successes of humanity
have, in many minds, made God,
or any idea of God,
redundant.

For man has conquered Everest
and reached out into space;
mastered many vile diseases,
conceived a baby in a tube;
travelled faster still than sound
and dived into the deepest sea;
and man has made the biggest bomb
to store away in case of war;
sufficient death for all the world,
on top of all the active waste
bequeathed to generations still unborn;
and man has made thalidomide,
dug for oil beneath the sea,
polluted many ocean shores,
poisoned birds and trees and fish.

Is man, the greatest, still so great
when godless frailties mark his way?

There are countless more
who find it hard
if not impossible
to believe in a loving God
with murder and massacre,
execution and torture,
oppression and racism,
apartheid,

and thousands upon thousands
of acts of cruelty and terror
which are done each day
in the name of government
and justice
and liberation
and reform
and even religion.

And there are those
who cannot bring themselves to faith
in a loving God
with earthquake, flood and drought.

Yet it is easy to apportion blame on God,
for that takes all the blame from man;
and man is still a fallen being,
still so failing in his living,
fallible in all his acts;
never could he be considered
the perfect ruler of all things
nor the wisest of all beings.

So there has to be a God,
there must be something greater
than anything that man can be
or do
or create.
The spiritual dimension to our living
is essential to understanding
the perfection of creation,
the potential of humanity,
the possibility of life.

The awareness of that dimension
is the beginning of faith.

Lord,
from our human nothingness
lift us up;
give us a vision of the what-might-be
in us
and all creation;
help us to believe
in ourselves,
in mankind,
and, most of all,
in you.

Open our eyes
our hearts and our lives
to your will
O Lord our God.
Amen.

CHOICE

There are two sides of God.

There is the God who wants the world
to be subject to his will
because he knows the frailties
humanity has brought;
and knows, without his guidance,
creation must be lost;
the God who wills the brotherhood
of every human being,
the end of war and greed and hate,
of evil men and evil ways,
the triumph of all good;
he is the caring, loving God
longing ever still
to take creation by the hand
and lead us all to love;
he is the God the Psalmist found
in every place he sought to go,
always there to help,
always there to care;
the God whose love is symbolised
on Christ's cross at Calvary;
That Cross was real,
its pain was felt;
God's love is real
but . . .

The other side of God

is that he wills men to be free
to do their will
if that's their wish
without recourse to him.

So we are free to pledge our faith
or not believe
just as we choose.

It is a freedom
to decide action,
to make policy
and that means
it can become a freedom
to be cruel and oppressive,
foolish and destructive;
the failures are not God's failures
they are always man's.

It is this freedom
which makes possible all the ill
that man can do;
for man's greatest frailty
is pride in his own success;
he takes the place of God;
creates the creator in the image of man
and then, disaster . . .
When sorrow comes
or danger
or tragedy or death
he has no hand to hold him,
no God to save his fall.

But God is there regardless,
if not to save his fall

to pick him up again
and dust him down
and set him on his way afresh,
still with his freedom
and his right
to choose himself – or God.

Faith is the choice that sets our course
towards our destiny
to walk with God
and know his help, his comfort and his strength
to share his service and his love;
not to believe is to choose
to try to live our life alone
and trust in our weak human power;
to find our discontent and hate
when things don't fall the way we wish;
to envy and to grasp in greed
and die without eternity.

Some choice!

Yet choice it is
and we must make it.
And if we choose God,
it will not be the God
of the stunning sunset
or the mighty view;
it will be the God who created us,
who reaches behind the facade
of what we pretend to be,
down into the depths of our being,
to the deepest point
where you are really you
and at that point,

possesses us,
impinging on the every detail
of our living;
loving us, yes, but demanding
standards and attitudes
beyond our believing,
controlling our freedom,
directing it constructively
to his glory
and our contentment.

Lord,
we cry to you
from the depths of our being;
without you
something is missing,
our joy is short-lived,
our sorrow is all-consuming,
our peace is but a brief pause
in our battle for living,
and our love is fleeting.

With you
we would be complete.

Yet, Lord,
we wander, incomplete,
lest we should lose our freedom
in finding you.
Reassure us,
remind us of the Christ
and the promise of life
lived to the full.

Be to us, Lord,
a true Father:
training,
restraining,
completing,
fulfilling us;
that we may be released
to reach our full potential
in this world
and the next.

Come, Lord God,
and help us choose you
now.
Amen.

SINGING

The Lord says:

Be still and know
that I am God;
supreme among the nations;
supreme over the world.

That's our problem.
Life is fast,
noisy,
busy,
complicated,
full of pain
and worry,
hatred
and jealousy
and all those things
that prove God isn't.

Our world has drawn a curtain
over the possibility of God
and now we say by action
if not by word:
There is no God;
and salve our troubled mind
because there is no evidence,
no hard scientific fact
that the Eternal One,
God,

is there – or here;
no mighty rushing wind
with cloven tongues of fire;
not even
a still small voice
of calm.

If only,
if only we knew how to listen
for God,
there is no doubt,
no doubt at all
that we would hear him
in every word of love,
in every breath of life;
if only we knew how to listen
we would hear our Lord say
that he is close beside us
all the way,
everywhere,
and always.

Sing to the Lord
all the world;
Worship the Lord with joy;
Come before him
with happy songs;
The Lord is good;
His love is eternal
and his faithfulness lasts for ever.

There it is again:
a word,
so out of touch,
so far from reality.

What is there to sing about?
What right have we to sing?
Where is God's love?
Where signs of his faithfulness?

There is war — the flower of youth
being torn and bloodied
— is that a time to sing?

There is hunger — famine for the many,
food in plenty for the few
and we are the few
— is that a time to sing?

There is oppression — race against race,
faith against faith,
nation against nation,
— is that a time to sing?

There is a discontent — in industry,
in community, in families,
unemployment and uncertainty,
violence and vandalism,
addiction and alcoholism,
purposelessness and permissiveness,
pornography and promiscuity,
— is that a time to sing?

If only we knew how to hope;
to catch a single glimpse of God
that makes hope a certainty
and the future a time for song;
if only, looking back
we could see just once
the hand of God at work in us

and then look forward
with that certainty and hope,
we would hear his word
and sing.

Lord,
slow us down,
help us to pause
even for a moment
from the busyness of the world
and the frenzy of our lives;
help us to catch our breath
from the breathlessness of living
and breathe from you
the breath of life anew.

Lord,
in the middle of the noise
that is the heartbeat and the pain
of living in our world
help us to be still,
silent,
relaxed,
expectant,
to hear your voice.
Then, Lord,
speak to us of certainty,
of coolness and of peace;
stir in our hearts
a song of faith
and of commitment
that sees beyond the darkness
to everlasting light.

Lord,
give us hope that is eternal
and harmony that will last for ever.

Always be full of joy in the Lord.
I say it again:
Rejoice!
Let everyone see
that you are unselfish and considerate
in all you do.
Remember that the Lord is coming soon.
Don't worry about anything;
Instead, pray about everything;
Tell God your needs
and don't forget to thank him
for his answers.

If you do this
you will experience God's peace
which is far more wonderful
than the human mind can understand.

Yes,
It is a time for singing.

SERVING

God says:

The kind of service I want
is that you stop oppressing
those who work for you
and treat them fairly
and give them what they earn.
I want you to share your food
with the hungry
and bring right into your homes
those who are helpless,
poor and destitute.
Clothe those who are cold
and don't hide from relatives
who need your help.

The Bible has done it again:
hit the nail on the head,
put the ball back in our court,
placed responsibility
firmly where it ought to be
on us.

All those things
which challenge God's love,
which make it difficult,
even impossible to believe,
all those things are back to us,
our fault,

back on our plate
for us to cope with.

Stop oppressing indeed!
Of course we don't.
Why then is there discontent,
why so many on the dole?
Is every wage a fair wage?
Are all conditions fair enough?
The labourer is worthy of his hire
but is the hire as worthy of his skill?
Well,
Is oppression just a myth?
God asks the question
but the buck stops with us.

Feed the hungry!
Fair enough,
but where we live
there aren't any hungry
to be fed.
Maybe not,
but while a third of humankind
eats twice our share
of the world's food
and we are in that third,
there will always be
hungry to be fed;
so when we say,
Why does a God of love
let children starve
and parents die from lack of food?
Remember it is not God
who made the imbalance

of the world's resources;
the buck stops with us.

Clothe the cold!
Shelter the homeless!
But aren't there organisations
geared up to do just that?
Is that not their job
and would they not be angry
if we should play a part?
Yet while a single baby
has no roof above its head
and tiny feeble fingers
turn blue and black from cold
and these things happen
both here and far away,
no organisation can remove
the pin-pricks of our heart,
for the buck stops with us.

And as for our relations,
that is the final straw.
Whoever wrote the word of God
knew nothing of our family scene.
No.
Nor did he need to.
For as long as we are able
our flesh and blood are ours;
and when there is some need
the buck stops with us.

It is a matter of love
this kind of serving
which is the will of God.

If only we knew how to love,
really to love,
as Jesus loved;
not soft sentimentalism,
not hot sensuality,
not even warm affection,
but the deep, costly,
giving-of-ourselves
in care and compassion.
If only we knew how to love like that
the world would become
a wonderful home.

Dear friends! Let us love one another,
for love comes from God.
Whoever loves is a child of God
and knows God,
for God is love.

I have learned how to get along happily
whether I have much, or little;
I know how to live on almost nothing,
or with everything;
I have learned the secret of contentment
in every situation.

I can do everything
with the help of Christ
who gives me strength and power.

That is the secret,
that is the power:
the ability to be content
whatever situation may arise,
be it plenty or shortage

riches or poverty
is found in Jesus Christ
the source of possibility.
So the buck which stops with us
is carried on by Christ
and the only buck we have to take
is the decision
and the sacrifice
of giving ourselves to him.

That is the beginning
and the middle
and the end
of serving.

Lord,
accept us as we are;
give us the common sense
to place our lives
into your care
that we may have the strength
and the love
to face the evils of the world
and by our caring
ease them
and in our serving
find the secret of contentment.
Amen.

LIVING

It's good to be alive!

The brand-new car
was going well
in the fast lane of the motorway.
At sixty-five
the distance between Glasgow
and a meeting in Edinburgh
is little more than an hour.

And, then, it happened;
across the carriageway in front,
impossible to believe,
a van doing a U-turn.
It's against the law
so it cannot happen,
but it did.
Late reaction,
because it was impossible,
then scream of brakes,
a bang a million miles away;
slow concertina of the car,
strong seat-belt arms
restraining body moves
holding it firm in the high-back seat,
secure,
like a baby in a mother's arms;
then, silence,
except the ticking of the clock.

It took a while to understand,
to comprehend the fact
the twisted, tangled mass of steel
was once a motor car;
and from the wreckage
facing back the way it came
to step out unscathed
save for a fractured wrist.

It's good to be alive!

And then it dawned
that time had hardly passed;
the whole thing happened in a flash,
it seemed to take so long;
the bonnet slowly folded up,
the dust hung gently in the air;
the van had taken hours of time
to cross the other carriageway
and come, at last, to rest
against a fence
beside a roadside field.
Eternity had passed,
but seconds in reality.
There was no time to think
of family or home,
of life or death or anything,
except to watch in disbelief
that this should come to me;
there was no time to put affairs
to right with man – or God.
It frightens and it terrifies,
but
it's good to be alive!

Of course,
many have experienced
such sudden face-to-face with death,
through accident or disease,
and some have not come through;
but those who do
discover what they knew deep down
but never really thought about:
that life is very special,
precious,
a fragile flower
to be cherished
and enjoyed,
but never to be wasted.

It's good to be alive,
to love one's wife and family,
to work and play and serve.
For when that life we take of right
is brought so near to death
it gives a special, vital sense
of having borrowed time;
of living on beyond the day
when death came first to call.
Each dawn is new
and fresh
and dear;
each breath a breeze of life
which we must share with every one,
that all the world
may meet each day
as new,
untouched by human ill,
unsoiled by human hate,
still in its chiffon wrapping

of the morning mist,
pristine in appearance
as in possibility;
and reach out in the peace
of nature's morning chorus
to make each new day
the best of all.
So may we remember always
the frailty of being,
and turn each moment of each day
over to our God
the source and strength of being.

Lord,
we remember our humanity,
the weakness of body,
the unwisdom of mind,
the feebleness of spirit,
and ask for your forgiveness.

We thank you, Lord,
for all the times
we've touched the door of death
and found it locked,
keeping us, for a while longer,
among our family and friends.
Help us when the lock is turned
and the door opens at our touch,
to pass through,
into your presence,
there to say with confidence,
in heaven as on earth,
It's good to be alive!

Lord,
into your care and protection
we give ourselves.
From the dying,
banish fears of death;
to the living,
give new joy of life;
for the traveller,
provide wisdom and safety;
and to us all,
give your peace.
Amen.

CHILDREN

Jesus said:

*Unless you change
and become like children
you will never enter
the Kingdom of Heaven.*

Surely he never said that!
He must have been mad
or a little off form
to say we must change
and become like children
if we want a future
in the hereafter.

After all,
children are trouble.
They fill the house
with perpetual motion,
dirty clothes,
lumps of mud
and decibels of noise;
they grow and fight
and try by any means
not to be a help
except when under pressure
or to get a *quid pro quo*.

To be like that

is a passport to paradise?
Surely not.
So what did he mean?

Well,
the noise and the trouble
that seem to surround
our children
are only part of the story;
for no-one can love
as a child can love,
even healing a hurt
they cannot understand;
and few can care
with the passionate care
of a child for a friend
or a pet;
and none are dependent
as a child depends
on his parents and teachers and friends
in the absolute way
that God wills of us
but only finds in a child.

And more . . .

Take any group of youngsters;
put them together
in amenable surroundings,
give them music of their kind
and challenge them to talk and think
about their life and what it means;
they will respond
beyond our hopes and fears;
they're enthusiastic

and energetic;
and they challenge all those things
we adults hold so dear,
not simply to destroy them,
but to make us justify them
for their generation
as well as ours:
our views on sex, morality,
on God and on the Church;
the way we speak in clichés
and pious words with little love;
they make us think and think themselves
for in that constant noise of 'pop'
their minds are rarely blank.
Of course they have no answers
but questions by the score
we should have asked before.

It's very hard to reconcile
the naughty, loving, growing child
with the young adult he becomes,
to recognise his views,
to realise that she's mature,
that neither is a little child
but fellow-adults
to be consulted not commanded,
to be our friends, not children
any more.

It's very hard for growing youth,
rebelling in their growing up,
testing all the standards
their parents set before them
against the world in which they live
and the future they must rule;

it's very hard for them as well
to recognise their father's law
and mother's care
is really love protecting them
from the first cold shocks of living
in the world outside the home.

So tensions rise and tempers fray,
but, where love is true,
a new respect begins to grow
across the generation void
and binds the wounds with understanding
making each one realise
both young and old
the oneness that is true.

To hear a new-born baby's cry,
to hold his tiny form,
is to wonder at the possibility
locked in the helpless form;
to see that child become a man
is satisfaction sure;
to know that each new stage of life
has got a parent's love
on which to build
is confidence untold.

So Jesus said:
Become like that
with God as our father;
dependent, loving, obedient child,
becoming friend and confidant;
in this way as our own children
releasing all the great potential
built into our creation.

Lord,
we thank you for children,
for their love
and their possibilities,
their enthusiasm
and their passion for causes.
Bless them in their growing
and becoming
that they may further your purpose
for our world.

Lord,
make us like them
dependent and obedient
to you
that we may become
what you created us to be
for Jesus' sake.
Amen.

BUSYNESS

Strange, isn't it,
how our experience is shaped by busyness
and pressure
and rarely punctuated
by pauses and peace?

Strange how every week
seems to be the week
when everything seems to happen;
when we seem to be rushing everywhere;
when everyone seems to call
and demand attention;
when, even when we are alone
and the work is done
and everything is quiet
we still persist in busyness.

Strange, isn't it,
how there never seems to be
a middle way
between pace and peace.

Even when we are on holiday
when we are out for rest and refreshment,
for renewal and re-creation,
even then
it's a rush to get there
and at the end
it's an equal rush to get home again;

we tie ourselves up
into balls of trouble on the roads,
caravans of caravans,
queues of crawlers
and tattered tempers.

Well,
You know what your day has been like,
its busyness or its quietness;
its round of activity
or its burden of loneliness
and suddenly you come to the point
when you want to stand up and shout:
Stop!
Enough!
Stop the world, I want to get off.
But you can't get off,
the clock will not stop,
each day gives way to the next
with precision and relentlessness;
No, you can't get off;
but you *can* stop;
you can stop the memories
good or bad
of the past;
you can stop the prospect
fair or foul
about the future
about tomorrow and tomorrow;
you can stop
take stock
and wait on God.

So you shall gather strength
to cope with your past

and to face your future,
your tomorrow.

Have you ever stood
on the top of a hill
or out in the middle of a wide open plain
and felt the wind on your face
and let the weight of the world
fall completely from your back?
That's prayer.

Have you ever listened
to the sound of strings
and let the tears roll down your face
to wash away the tension
and the terrors of the day?
That's prayer.

Take a look at the Bible.
It tells about men
and their meeting with God.
Moses on the mountain
apart from his fellows
apart from the pressure of running the Exodus,
there was God.
And all the prophets have had their dreams,
their visions of what might be,
their visions of what would be,
they had their visions in the desert
in the wilderness
apart
and there was God.
John the Baptist found his ministry
apart from all the comforts of this world
in the wilderness.

And Jesus himself
not just after his baptism
but all through his ministry
went apart from the world
got away
somewhere
where the pressure that lay heavy on his mind
where the things that troubled him
where everything
could not reach
and there he waited for the word
and the counsel of the Father.
And that was how he taught his disciples
to take time to think
to be still
and listen for God.
So let us do likewise;
and in the busyness of our lives
take time to be still
and know that God is with us;
and listen for him.

Lord,
you know our life;
its busyness,
its loneliness,
its tensions,
its terrors,
its troubles,
its tiredness;

you know the weariness
that burrows deep into the bones;
you know the lethargy
that hangs heavy on our head;

you know the loneliness
that builds barriers around us;

Lord,
give us freedom from our prison
and peace
real peace
now
and for ever.
Amen.

EVENING

Abide with us
for it is towards evening
and the day is far spent.

Evening
is a time for reflection;
when the blue of the sky pales
and grey-brown cotton clouds
float gently
reflecting the dying embers
of the sun
in reds and crimson,
gold and lemon,
until the pale mist of dusk
begins to hide the view
and birds are silent,
stillness falls,
street lights begin to glisten
and day is done.

Evening
is a time when all the pressures of the day
have a chance, at least, to ease,
when troubles fall slowly from the mind,
when bodies rest
relaxing in a favourite chair
easing pain and weariness
preparing for the sleep
of the coming night.

Evening
is a time for renewal,
a time to play,
to entertain, be entertained,
to let sweet music
or drama
or quiet fireside company
remake our lives,
soften the hardness of the day,
ease the pain of words
or decisions,
give the being time
to recover, ready for tomorrow.

Evening
is a time for slowing down,
for easing the pace,
for rest.

So, evening is about life.
At birth,
we are at the dawn;
in youth,
the morning;
in middle years,
noon-tide;
and then the day of life
begins to fade
until the later years
are the evening of our days.

And that is right.

For as the evening
in our living

restores us for tomorrow
with rest for the body,
peace for the mind,
forgiveness for the conscience,
renewal for the spirit,
so the evening of the whole of life
with retirement
and the slowing down
of all our faculties
is the time of preparation
for the new tomorrow
in the new world
in the morning.

Have you ever taken time
to look long and silently
at the dusk?
Far beyond the skyline
of the houses
across the railway from home,
behind the church spire
rising above the houses that surround it;
the hills that stretch both west and south
from Edinburgh
are just a blue-grey line
under the gathering clouds
against which
the flashing lights of the Forth Road Bridge
shine an ever-brightening red.
Suddenly
all's well with the world;
peace is possible
if only for a moment.

If this day has been a good one,

let the evening bless that goodness;
if this day has brought some sorrow,
let the evening comfort that sadness;
if this day has been difficult,
let the evening ease that trial;
because evening,
when the day is done
is time to spend
at one with God.

So let us pray.

Lord,
At the end of the day
as gentle clouds
point the way they wish to go,
we point ourselves
to spend some time apart with you.

The evening is our assurance
that you have ordered our world —
light and dark,
night and day,
rain and shine.

So, Lord,
we put our hand
in your hand
that your touch
may give courage, comfort and care;
wiping every tear,
restoring hope
and faith
and love.

Lord,
into your safekeeping
we place the evening of this day
and the evening of our days
that we may know your presence
always.

Amen.

LOVE

Jesus said:

*Love one another
just as I have loved you.*

If only we could
learn to love
as Jesus loved —
that all-consuming care
possessing his attention . . .

A blind man by the roadside,
a woman in the crowd,
someone with a withered hand
in church,
an epileptic boy,
a centurion's servant,
a churchman's child;
every time
only the one in need
was the centre of his attention.

That is love,
real love,
more than the cuddle-comfort
of a mother for her child,
holding her baby tightly
to her breast;
more than the arms-entwined

and body-touching love
of lovers;
more than the sacrificial love
of son or daughter
for aged parent;
all of which is love
but not the Jesus love.

To love as Jesus loved
is to lose oneself in love,
to see no other end but love;
to make oneself as nothing
so that the one to be loved
takes all the world,
the centre of the stage.

How difficult it is.

When we are occupied
at work or conversation
or concentrating on a thought,
to be disturbed
distracted or diverted
by someone in need
is often irritation —
but it is love.

When someone does us wrong,
maligns our name,
damages our reputation,
says hurtful things behind our back,
abuses trust
and steals our goods,
to forgive
and to forget

because forgiving means forgetting
and starting fresh,
to forgive
is often hard –
but it is love.

When someone in sore need
rejects our hand of help
refuses any charity,
denies the need itself
berates our care,
to go again and still again
until the need is admitted
the care accepted,
the problem solved
is often too much to ask –
but it is love.

Love is patient;
Love is kind and envies no-one;
Love is never boastful,
> *nor conceited,*
> *nor rude,*
> *never selfish,*
> *not quick to take offence.*
Love keeps no score of wrongs,
> *does not gloat over other men's sins*
> *but delights in the truth.*

There is nothing love cannot face;
There is no limit to its faith
> > *its hope*
> > *its endurance.*

Love will never come to an end.

Do you remember
the refreshing shock of a cold shower?
Or the first splash of a morning wash
before the water has run hot in the tap?
Or the dive into a mountain pool?
Or the trouser-turned-up-tip-toe into the tide?
After the shock
and the cold,
that mysterious
comforting,
glorious, exciting, invigorating, renewing warmth?
That's what the love of God is like:
forgiving,
caring,
comforting,
restoring,
always;

Like the sea
splashing forever on the shore,
on every shore.

Lord,
drown us in your love.
Lift us on the waves of your spirit
that, in touch with your love,
we may be renewed and restored;
and, being restored,
may be released from our unloveliness
to love as Jesus loved
that his love may have its ancient power
in our day
through us
and fill our world,
our nation,

our city,
our street,
our house,
now.

The Lord bless you and keep you;
The Lord make his face to shine upon you
    and be gracious unto you;
The Lord lift up the light of his countenance upon
you
    and give you his peace.

Amen.

REMEMBRANCE

Each Saturday of Remembrance
the Albert Hall
is filled to capacity
in the presence of the Queen.
Cadets and Captains,
colours, combatants and Chelsea Pensioners,
nurses, seamen, flyers and observers;
a whole nation of uniforms,
military and civilian,
stand in silence
as poppy petals fall
slowly,
abundantly;
every one a life
lost,
but remembered.

Each Sunday of Remembrance
there is pomp, ceremony and silence
at the Cenotaph;
wreaths and bugles,
flags and swords,
again the Queen,
her ministers and Parliament,
her Forces and her people
stand
to remember.

To remember what?

The mud and misery of Mons
a diamond jubilee of years ago
or the flames of Coventry and Clydebank
a generation on;
or is it nearer still,
Afghanistan, the Middle East
and dear beloved Ireland?

Is it to remember
the Unknown Soldier
and the latest Ulster death
and in between
millions of loved-ones lost
loved still, but lost
in the madness of men's wars?

Is that remembrance?
Two minutes from a nation's year,
given now only by some
in formal recognition
of service to the end?

Or is it simply sentiment
or glory of the fight
as if to die in war
was nobler far
than for a child
swept off by flood
in peace?

If there are things to remember,
surely they must be
the inhumanity and greed,
the passion for power and fame,
the prejudice and vanity

that made the wars
that killed so many.

If there are things to remember,
surely they must be
a flush of shame
that lives so newly grown,
so near their peak of greatness,
so vital for the future
were torn from the world.
No sentimental glow of giving.
They didn't want to die;
their lives were snatched away;
their greatness lay
in their obedience and devotion
through all their fear
right to the end.

If there are things to remember.
surely they must be
that somewhere
even in the deepest human hell and folly
there is life and love
and hope.

For that's what remembrance is about:
the good,
the possible,
the faith,
the sacrifice,
not just in war,
but in life itself.

And at the heart of that remembrance —
God.

Remembrance is about remembering,
about not forgetting,
not taking for granted,
or lightly,
our heritage
and the word of God.

God said:
Thou shalt not kill.

God said:
*Beware lest you forget
the Lord your God.*

Beware.

Remember.

If only we had done this
would there have been
a Mons or a Hiroshima,
a Soweto or a Belfast?

If only we will do this
what could our future become?
For to remember God
even in the smallest things
is to turn the future
upside-down.

Lord,
help us to remember
and not forget
that you are Lord
of the present
and forever.

So, turn our world upside down:
for pain, give comfort;
for sorrow, give trust
that leads to joy;
for war and division, give peace
and simple mutual respect;
for hate, give love;
for all our uncertainties,
give a measure of confidence;
for all the things that disturb us,
give us the assurance that you will provide;
and for the restlessness of the day,
give us
and all our loved ones
sleep and serenity.

Amen.

FORGIVENESS

Jesus said:

If you forgive others
the wrongs they have done to you,
your Father in heaven
will also forgive you.
But if you do not forgive others,
then the Father will not forgive
the wrongs you have done.

Forgiveness matters.

It matters to children
whose process of learning
and growing
is punctuated by mistakes
and naughtiness
testing the limits of patience
and temper.
Once the limit is past
and punishment or reprimand
the sentence carried out,
forgiveness matters.
It is the healing,
the restoring of relationship,
the reconciling word
that makes the future possible.

It matters to us all

whose natural humanity
is fallible and frail.
A single second of human error
in a lifetime of inerrancy
if such was possible
can lay an unbearable burden
of guilt and remorse,
a painful memory of death or disaster
forever on a mind and soul
without forgiveness.
It matters
for it is the only antidote for guilt
which covers up the scars,
the open wounds of memory.

It matters to God.
For this he sent his son
to make forgiveness
for all men's wrong
a living possibility.
That's what the Cross
is all about —
forgiveness;
how much it costs,
how much it matters.

It was not without significance
when the paraplegic man
was lowered through the roof
for Jesus to heal
that Jesus said first,
Your sins are forgiven
and then,
Take up your bed and walk.

Forgiveness
is real wholeness,
the completeness of the soul
which for eternity
is more important than physical wholeness
for the body we shall leave behind.
The wholeness comes
because forgiveness and forgetting
go hand in hand.

Forgiveness
means a clean sheet,
a new start,
a forgotten past.
Without that amnesia
it is not forgiveness.

How often do we say
we will forgive
but not forget?
Our forgiveness is meaningless.

How often do we say
we have forgiven,
but keep a store of wrongs
safe in our memory
filed for the future
to be cast up
at an opportune moment?
That forgiveness, too, is meaningless.

How often do we determine
never to forgive some wrong,
some word or act
often unintended, accidental

or simply thoughtless
but sometimes deliberate,
which hurt?
Yet not to forgive
is to separate ourselves for ever
from family
from friends,
from God.

Yes, it is hard to forgive
for forgiving demands forgetting;
and it is hard to accept forgiveness
for acceptance hurts our pride;
neither is easy
but both are essential
if we would follow Christ.
Seventy times seven
is a lot of forgiving and being forgiven.
But remember:
God's forgiveness of us
depends on our forgiving each other.

Lord,
forgive our unwillingness to forgive
and be forgiven.
Help us to recognise our wrong
and accept forgiveness
and forgive ourselves.
Give us the love
which keeps no score of wrongs
but obliterates the memory
of evil and mistake
and sets the record right.

Teach us, Lord,

how to forgive each other
that we might be forgiven
by you.
Lift high the Cross before us
that we may see the cost
of your forgiving love
and respond in kind each day.
Help us to bury those wrongs
which have separated us for years
from loved ones,
from friends,
from you and from your Church,
through the forgiveness
you brought into our world.

Lord,
forgive us
for Jesus' sake.

Amen.

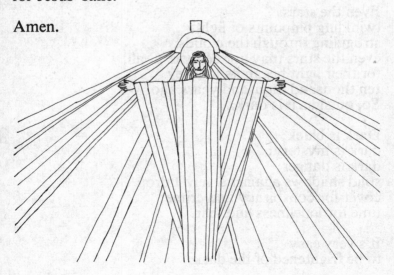

DARKNESS

Outside, it is dark.

Beyond the orange lights
through the window,
shining on the street below,
throwing grotesque shadows
through the trees
in the park across the way,
beyond the orange lights,
out over the Firth of Forth,
it is dark.

Even the stars,
twinkling pinpoints of light,
struggling through the clouds,
even the stars may not be there at all,
for their light began its journey
ten thousand thousand years ago.
So, outside, it is dark.

Dark is black;
dark is mystery;
dark is danger;
solid shadows against a velvet drop,
cover for conspiracy and crime;
time for loneliness and fear.

It's very easy
to be frightened of the dark;

to be apprehensive
of the dangers of the night.
Shadows on the wall from swinging curtains
take up grotesque and terrifying shapes;
and simple sounds of floorboards
clicking and creaking into place
make great explosions in the night.

Somehow,
over the centuries,
dark has been synonymous with sin;
with all the evil of the world.
The Devil is the Prince of Darkness;
Black Mass the antithesis of right.
And so the hours of dark
are sinister shadows on the days of life,
better spent in sleep,
forgotten,
escaped from.

Even the Bible
identifies the dark as gloom,
obscurity
and mystery.
Those who turn from God,
deny his will,
dispute his way,
are cast into outer darkness,
infinite blackness,
separated for eternity,
void of being.

The unknown
is shrouded in darkness
like the dark of deep waters.

As the sand of the shore
slopes away,
so the seas begin to lose their green
to the white-capped slate
of the deep,
hiding the secrets
of the world beneath the waves;
or like the black holes of the universe
sucking into their void
the galaxies around them
like a cosmic hoover
reducing worlds to dust
and everlasting nothingness.
Dark is gloom,
the shroud we draw around us
when we are low
or wish to hide our real self
from others in our world.

Dark is the colour
of furtiveness,
of less than honest life,
of secrets unrevealed,
of mystery maintained,
of doubt, despair and death.

Yet, dark is normal.
As the earth spins round the sun
some, at least, must lie in shadow,
shrouded in dark,
but only for a season,
a matter of hours.
Tomorrow will come;
the dawn will break;

the sun will shine,
if not from a cloudless sky,
or through the clouds,
above them;
light will replace the dark,
brightness throw new shadows,
less sinister and black,
and day will take the place of night
with undiminishing regularity,
not just once,
but always
and for ever.

Lord,
it is dark.
In our lives
the darkness is oppressive:
the sorrows and the strains of life itself
shroud us from the light;
deep shadows cast by pain and worry,
depression and dispeace,
the pressures of our work,
the tensions of our home;
the frustrations of unemployment,
the hindrance of infirmity,
the helplessness of watching loved ones
suffer pain and slip away;
the loss of trust,
the loss of love,
and deepest shade of all our shades
the growing loss of hope.

Lord,
remind us of the dawn
in all its morning glory

slowly and certainly
transforming the sombre blackness
of the night
into the triumphant brightness
of the day;
and let that certainty
of the ever-coming dawn
uphold us in our darker hours.

Lighten our darkness,
Lord.

Amen.

COLD

Outside, it is cold.

Edinburgh is built on hills;
The Georgian splendour
of the New Town
slopes down towards the Forth
in sweeping crescents,
majestic terraces and mews,
so that the unsuspecting walker,
stepping in the shelter of a mansion,
turns a corner
to face an icy blast of wind
worthy of the Pole;
so, as the frost begins to sparkle
on the roofs of cars
in the street below,
even the softest breeze
roughens the skin
and numbs the nose
in the twinkling of an eye.
All that at any time
save on the warmest summer eve.

In winter
when trees stretch out their barren branches
like arthritic fingers
pointing to the sky
look down through woolly clouds
from that sky

over the Atlantic
and see the ocean
first spotted with small flecks of white;
then larger islands
of solid ice
until the water waste
becomes a solid sea of ice
like marble,
its massive whiteness
veined in blue-black lines
as crevasses spread.

Even at the centre of the world
where north and south divide and meet
the equator splits the peaks
of Kirinyaga;
and while the land below
is bathed in sun
of tropical intensity
the snow lies deep
and cold
on the summit.

On land,
at sea,
in the air
cold is danger.

Cold is pain,
discomfort,
the awkwardness of heavy clothes,
the numbness of face and fingers,
tears in the eyes,
a struggle for life.

So is the coldness of a heart.
Indifference and disdain,
compassionlessness and bluntness.
It is the cause of pain,
of hate and resentment,
of retribution and dispeace.

How easy it is to be cold,
to dismiss another's need
as weakness
not to be encouraged;
to put aside all care
as waste.

How easy to reduce
a hopeful heart to tears
by just one glance
of ice-cold eyes.

How easy to reach
a peak of one's career
by riding rough-shod over others
in icy-cold indifference
and single-minded will.

How easy to be objective,
apart from others' cares,
spectating from afar
with cold, uncaring heart.

And all these things we do
to some degree,
on some occasion.
We lower the temperature
of love,

and bring the cold
of disinterest,
and cause the pain.

The cold of winter
and the wind
is a cold that penetrates
the warmest clothes.
The cold of heart
and of eye
is a cold that penetrates
the warmest love.

Cold is danger.

Yet if there is any certain thing
in this uncertain world
it is that after winter
spring will come;
that trees will change their barren arms
for foliage of summer green;
that birds will sing a new refrain
and sun will melt the snow
and warm the world.

There will always be spring
and summer
after every winter;
so it must be just as sure
that warmth can come
to the coldest heart,
even ours.

Lord,
it is cold.

The coldness in our life
is lack of love,
intolerance and hate,
our preference for prejudice,
our lust for power,
our selfishness and pride;
these are the minus temperatures
that freeze the fullness from our lives.

Lord,
let the fire of your love
melt the ice in our hearts
and release a warm refreshing flood
and pent-up goodness on the world.

Lord,
make us lovable and loving.
So lighten our darkness.

Amen.

QUIET

Outside, it is quiet.

All the noise of the day is over.
The traffic and the crowds
have deserted the city
for television, radio,
theatre and restaurant,
for home and bed;
now is the time of quiet,
of peace and restfulness.

But for many
quiet is silence,
the oppressive silence of loneliness;
and loneliness for some
brings apprehension and sadness,
memories of different times,
shadows of the evening of our days.

And there are other quietnesses.
There is the quiet,
the calm before the storm;
the pregnant stillness
waiting to give birth to noise;
the breathless peace
when not a single leaf can move,
and birds retreat
to silent expectation

and whispers magnify themselves
to mighty cries.

It is a frightening time,
like the breathless
peaceful calm
in the hurricane's eye,
waiting for the wind.

There is the quiet
of evening hills,
the sky too dark to see,
too light to show the stars;
the noise of day
replaced by tiny rustles in the grass,
short calls and cries
and silence.
Long silence.

There is the quiet
of contentment;
the silent company
by the dying embers of the fire;
the love unspoken,
the unity unsaid
but nonetheless complete.

There is the quiet
of contemplation,
the silent rehearsing of the thoughts
when all the difficulties
can find their context
in the confidence of will;
when new ideas are born,
considered

and remembered
for future reference and use.

In many ways
it is quiet.
Once the pace of life slows down
and time is on our hands,
to sit and stare
at the flames that flicker in the fire,
or stand and wonder
at the slow coming of the night
until the silent stars proclaim
the day is done
and night has come.

Yet, tomorrow, the silence of the world
will be broken with the sounds of living:
work and worship,
prayer and pleasure,
news and entertainment,
wind and storm;
for, as sure as the dawn follows the dark
and summer winter,
so the activity of life
follows the silence of the night;
traffic will fill the empty streets
and factory floors will rumble into life.

Lord,
it is quiet.
Our quietness is the secret fear,
the silent stillness of death
which comes so near
in quiet evening hours;

the unknown sleep
at the end of our days;
the mystery
that is our common destiny,
leading us away from what we know
to that which we can only hope for.

Lord,
let your presence in our quiet
remind us of your promises,
that, as the world will stir to life
after this night's sleep,
as the dawn leads on another day,
so the deep stillness of eternal sleep
will stir to new life
beyond the grave.

Remind us, Lord,
that as surely as the snowdrop
pushes through the winter ground
and tiny buds break out on barren stems,
as surely as the sun will shine again
we shall live again.

So, Lord,
send us to our rest in peace,
to dreamless sleep in certainty
that beyond the tensions
and troubles of this world
you are in control,
your peace is the quiet that enfolds us.

Uphold all who labour through this night
with strength sufficient for their work;
surround those who are ill and in pain

and those who watch with them
in their sleepless hours
with your deep, loving, peace.
Forgive the follies of this day,
restrain the evil of the night.

Into your hands, Lord, we commit our world,
our land,
our loved ones
and ourselves
and all the countless millions in the world
on whom,
unwitting and unthinking,
we depend for life.

Lighten our darkness, Lord,
and still our souls.

Amen.

WONDER

Wonder is wonderful.

Have you ever stood under the stars,
looked up and wondered,
thought about those suns and worlds,
and possibilities of life
out there on other planets?
Have you ever thought about
the light that travelled all those years,
millions of years
to touch your eyes that night?
Have you ever thought about
the galaxies
that race across the infinity of space,
the countless millions of stars
and unseen planets
and wondered at the mind
that planned and caused it all?

Have you ever taken time
to look in detail at a leaf,
to see the deep perfection of its form,
like something specially made,
created for itself,
fragile and frail
and limited in life?

Have you ever thought about
the fact of snow,

that no two flakes that fall
will ever be the same design;
like finger-prints
of the ten fingers
of all the millions
in every age,
no two will match
no two will be the same?

Have you ever stood
to watch a dawn or dusk,
the rising or the setting of the sun
the shifting shades
the clouds
the moods that they create?

Have you ever drawn breath
at all the mysteries of science,
the micro-chip,
the computer,
journeys to the fringe of space,
television pictures of other worlds,
machines and medicines
unknown, unheard of,
undiscovered,
inconceivable when we were born?

Have you ever looked at the miniature perfection
of a new born baby:
the wrinkled face,
the tiny fingernails,
the angry look
from being so suddenly
and unceremoniously

thrust from the warm comfort of the womb
into this strange world of giants?
And have you seen
the looks of wonder in a baby's eyes
at simple ordinary things
like the sound of a rattle,
the shape of a ball,
the flutter of a butterfly?

Wonder is wonderful.

But what happens to it?
Soon – too soon it seems –
the objects of our wonder
become the simple facts
of every day;
it is no cause to wonder any more
that men have walked upon the moon
and orbit now
above the earth;
it is no cause to wonder now
that Wimbledon is watched
by four hundred million souls
across the world
precisely as it happens.
Science and astronomy,
medicine and psychology
have taken from experience
the need for wonder
and so our world seems less exciting,
less wonderful.

To wonder
is to stand in awe,
to pause

and see ourselves in context,
to recognise
the guiding hand and master-plan
of a Creator,
to accept
each stepping stone
of scientific discovery
on earth or in outer space
for what it is,
a step towards the destiny of man
to be like God.

To wonder
is to stand in awe,
to let the majesty of hills,
the endless rollers of the sea,
the glory of the spectrum,
of colour and of shade,
the thrill of natural sound
of birds and animals,
of orchestra and solo voice,
the feel of wind upon the face
and sun upon the back
or rain upon the head,
to let all that remind us
of our own humanity
our smallness and our frailty
and yet our great potential
for good within the world.

Lord,
restore to us
the capacity for wonder.
Help us to wonder at your creation

and at your love for us;
let our wonder never cease,
but inspire us
to place ourselves
within your master-plan
and let your will direct us
that we may be part
of the wonder that surrounds us.

May our eyes never be dulled
to beauty and to love
nor so caught up with things of the world
that we cannot see
things of eternity.

Lord,
may each day for us
be a voyage of new discovery
and wonder
as it was when we were children;
for without that
the kingdom of heaven is hard to reach.

Amen.

A WORD FOR LIVING

In the beginning there was nothing.
In the very beginning,
before the universe,
the solar systems and the galaxies came to be,
in the very beginning
there was nothing.

Void.

And then, the void became matter;
and the matter took form;
and the form took life;
and the life became you
and me.
And we,
we do, take, become, make — what?
That's the ultimate question.
In the long process of creation,
of coming into being,
of coming to be,
what is our place or destiny?
Our purpose?
Our right or reason to be,
to breathe the ever scarcer air,
to eat the ever precious food,
to burn the ever lessening stock
of this world's energy and resource?
What is our right?

God said: Now we will make human beings;
They will be like us and resemble us;
They will have power over the fish, the birds
And all animals, domestic and wild, large and small.
So God created human beings,
Making them to be like himself.
He created them male and female, blessed them and
said:
Have many children
So that your descendants will live over the earth
And bring it under their control.
I am putting you in charge of the fish,
The birds and all the wild animals.

Stewards!
That's what we are,
or are meant to be.
Stewards of the form and shape,
the loveliness of creation.

It's very easy to believe in God
out there among the hills,
where soft grey chiffon mist
stretches its inquisitive fingers
into the forest firs,
or where the mighty ocean wave
explodes into a rainbow shower of spray
against the towering cliff,
in almost senseless anger and frustration;
yet, every day and century,
carves out its latest imagery
around our stormy shore.

It's very easy to believe in God
at the first cry of a new-born babe,

or the mystery of bud becoming bloom,
or when the first few streaks of lightening grey
across an azure sky at night
assure us of another dawn,
or when the winter snows give way at last
to some few silver waterfalls and sun.

It's easy to believe that God exists,
the very beginning of all this;
the source of all our being;
of life itself,
and love;
and that which drives us on
to what is still to come,
with expectation and with hope,
that what we are and do and make
has some more value than itself alone.

It's easy to accept the possibility
that, out beyond the mystery of being,
there is a reason and an order to it all,
which, for convenience and simplicity,
to bind us all in common right,
we call God;
and we believe
or say we do,
as men have done in every age
to make some sense of being,
believed in God,
the source of being
and the ultimate concern of all that being.

Without that faith,
that anchor for our lives,
to live is to exist;

to work is to survive;
to be is to happen,
a flash,
a faintest flicker in the eye of eternity,
a speck of irritation,
there
and gone,
forgotten and unremembered,
unmourned.

With that faith
in God,
there is a reason and a hope,
a value to our living;
to be the stewards of creation
and to hope ourselves a part
of the eternity from whence we came –
the time before the void
that was the beginning
and the time that will be for ever
when time is, for us, no more.

With that faith in God
and even with our feeble comprehension
of the possibility of life,
we are responsible,
the faithful in every age,
for stewardship and service
that all the world's resources
of men
and of those things which maintain human life –
food and fire,
warmth and energy,
shelter and justice,
peace and prosperity;

we are, as God's people,
responsible for them.

And what do we make of them?
Just this:

I looked at the earth . . . it was a barren waste;
    at the sky . . . there was no light.
I looked at the mountains . . . they were shaking;
    and the hills were rocking to and fro.
I saw that there were no people;
    even the birds had flown away.
The fertile land had become a desert;
    its cities were in ruins.
The Lord has said that the whole earth
    will become a wilderness.
    The earth will mourn;
    The sky will grow dark;
The Lord has spoken and will not change his mind;
He has made his decision and will not turn back.
At the noise of the horsemen and bowman
    everyone will run away;
    some will run to the forest,
others will climb up among the rocks;
    every town will be left empty
and no one will live in them again . . .
    You are doomed!

The stark description
of a nuclear holocaust, perhaps?
Or the failure of our human race
to place the priorities of stewardship
in their proper order,
so that the power over the world,
which is God's gift of creation,

takes precedence over the care of people?
Or just the sheer madness of mankind
tearing itself asunder
by riot and by war,
by greed and the injustice
that breeds cruelty and hate,
that makes men the oppressors
of their equals under God?
(You see, it comes again
in every human act,
when God is left aside
there's no possibility of right.)
No. Those words were not addressed
to our day and generation;
they were the stark prediction
of the prophet Jeremiah
some two and a half thousand years ago.
But don't let that deceive you
into a false sense of security;
for if there ever was a time
when the predictions of Jeremiah
and his fellow-prophets
had a collective ring of truth,
it is in our own time.

It is quite extraordinary
that in our time
there should be so much tension and violence,
so much blatant hatred and oppression,
so much torture and greed,
so much plain prejudice and dishonesty,
bitterness and need,
so much injustice and quite massive imbalance
of this world's goods;
it is quite unacceptable

that we stagger on
undermining our affluent economy
with greed-born industrial unrest,
refusing to do a decent day's work
for a decent wage
and, by so doing,
depressing the economy
so that others less fortunate than us
are rendered workless,
unemployed,
on the dole,
deprived of dignity
and often, too, of hope.
Of course, there are the dole-men
who never want to work,
but the vast majority of the people of this land
are perfectly willing
to work their hearts out
for their wage and their dignity.
It is quite impossible to understand
that we do all this
while above us shines the legend
that we are made like God,
that only in an understanding of God
can full life be possible;
and God's will is not that we should be divided
by class or creed,
by sex,
by riches and poverty
by boss and worker,
by any human prejudice or division;
God's will
and his plan for the success of the world
and of your life and mine
is mind-blowingly simple and possible:

That they may be one,
Us,
all of us,
brothers,
pulling together,
caring and serving.

Sloppy sentimental stuff it may seem
but we haven't really tried it yet,
so we cannot really tell.
But one thing is certain:
without God
we cannot make it.

What is the answer?
There is a promise:

God is our shelter and strength,
Always ready to help in times of trouble,
So we will not be afraid;
Even if the earth is shaken
And mountains fall into the ocean depths;
Even if the seas roar and rage
And the hills are shaken by violence.
The Lord Almighty is with us,
The God of Jacob is our refuge;
Come, and see what the Lord has done on earth:
He stops wars all over the world,
He breaks bows, destroys spears
And sets shields on fire.
Stop fighting, he says, and know that I am God,
Supreme among the nations,
Supreme over the world.
The Lord Almighty is with us,
The God of Jacob is our refuge.

Good point that –
The God of Jacob is our refuge:
Jacob made a bit of a mess of things;
he started out badly,
he stole his brother's birthright,
cheated him out of it,
encouraged by his mother, yes,
but he did it
and he paid for it;
he had to fight with the angel of the Lord;
he had to live with his hip out of joint;
but he found his God forgiving and empowering
and all that he had wanted when he stole
and spoiled the relationship of brotherhood
with his own greed and power wish,
all of it
and much much more
came to him, finally,
when, in that painful encounter,
he got right with God

But there is another point
in the mind of the Psalmist
and that is equally simple:
that God is ready to help
in the here and now,
not in the eternity to come,
but now,
in the today and tomorrow
that you and I will have to live.
Jesus underlined that promise
when St. Matthew has him say:
I am with you always
to the end of the age.
That's what the whole Gospel is about:

that there is a certainty
of the God-with-us;
not just the God of the beautiful sunset
and the baby's tiny finger-nail,
or the bumble bee's impossible flight,
or the orchid's priceless bloom;
not the God alone of poetry and music,
of art and architecture;
not even the God of mighty theologians' words,
but the ordinary, almighty,
eternal and infinite God-with-us
that Jesus tried to show:
the working God at the carpenter's bench,
the caring God at the feeding of the multitude,
the healing God in the touch of the robe,
the loving God with the children
and with Mary at the tomb
and with Martha and Mary;
the God who transformed the untransformable,
the taxmen Matthew and Zacchaeus,
the proud and unpredictable sons of Zebedee,
the big, brash, powerful fisherman, Peter,
the haughty academic, Paul;
and, down through every age and year,
a numberless army of forgiven folk
whose lives are changed in ways
no human will could bring about,
this God
stands at the door of our lives,
at the gate of our world,
waiting to be invited in,
waiting, in desperate fear,
that we might wait
until it is too late;
for all the predictions are

that, before this century has left us far behind
in our own dust of death,
the mushroom clouds of instant war
will, at a single stroke,
solve all the shortages of energy and food
by ending all the hopes of God
in holocaust;
or, if man's fear is sensitive
and saves him from the brink,
the greed will bring more hatred
and black will rise for justice
and pain will be the heritage
we leave to those who come after us.
Thus speak the prophets of today;
for as the accountants and financiers
build up their power in all things,
as money and its profit
takes precedence for all,
as small and family business
with service and a smile,
is swallowed up by multinationals
who, even now, own half the earth,
we people will be pawns
of inconsequential worth.
Don't think that I'm an Amos
and bounded in with doom;
these things are here already,
encroaching on our world
and God stands
still
beside us
waiting for the call
that can release upon our day
a power of good and love and peace
that never could be hoped for

or even imagined.
If only we could be bothered,
if only we will
for it is the only way.

Suppose we do?
Suppose we call in God,
invite him into his world,
into our lives,
into his creation,
for all are his;
suppose we open up
and let him in;
suppose we let him rule our lives,
what then?
What's in it for us?
What'll we get out of it?

Maybe that's not fair;
maybe that's a bit sacrilegious;
but that's the sort of language
that's commonplace these days;
and that's the sort of world
into which we'd be calling out for God;
so, just as there's no use dusting off the Bible
because the minister may call,
there's no point in pretending
things are other than they are
when we call the God of all of them
to sort them out among us.
So what's in it all, for us,
in the present and the future?
And what about the past mistakes
that all of us have made,
especially those deep secret ones

that only we and he will know?
What's in it?

The Lord says, The time is coming
when I will make a new covenant
with the people of Israel.
I will put my law within them
and write it on their hearts.
I will be their God
and they will be my people.
I will forgive their sins
and I will no longer remember their wrongs.

I will give them a new heart
and a new mind.

The troubles of the past
will be gone and forgotten.
I am making a new earth and new heavens.
The events of the past
will be completely forgotten.
Be glad and rejoice for ever
in what I create.

When anyone is joined to Christ
he is a new being;
the old has gone,
the new has come.

I saw a new heaven and a new earth.
The first heaven and the first earth disappeared
and the sea vanished.
And I saw the Holy City,
the new Jerusalem coming down out of heaven from
God;

I heard a loud voice speaking from the throne:
Now God's home is with mankind
He will live with them . . . and he will be their God;
He will wipe away all tears from their eyes;
There will be no more death;
The old things have disappeared.

Behold I make all things new.

What's in it for us?
Too much, perhaps, to comprehend.
For this is the beginning of a new order,
not the cleaning up of the old.
That is to be forgotten.
It is a real transformation,
a new creation that is on the cards.
Yes, there is forgiveness for the past,
total and complete,
and that's a promise;
yes, there is hope for the future,
but a greater hope than ever before
we let ourselves believe possible;
it is a hope that there really will be peace;
that there really will be brotherhood;
that there will be equality
and justice and truth and love;
above all, love.

Utopia?

Of course not!
It cannot be when it is a promise.
Yet, ultimately, it lies with us,
the opportunity to change the world.

It lies with us
because we first must make that act of commitment
that lets God create a new us,
here and now,
in the temporality of today
for the eternity of tomorrow;
it means that we have got to be
vehicles of love,
just that;
the love which is the servant of the weak,
the clothes to the naked,
the food to the hungry,
the shelter to the homeless,
the healing to the sick,
the freedom to the oppressed,
the justice for all mankind;
it is the love
which works for union not division,
which knows no barriers of colour,
nor creed nor social standing;
it is the love which never gets tired,
never gives up.
Yes, it's a tall order,
but as we have never given God a chance
to let it loose on us,
how can we say it is impossible?

You see the point of what we've done today
is in the three thoughts from which it grew:

In the beginning – God
In the middle of life – God
In the end and in eternity – God

But, only by request:

Lord,
In this hour of worship
clear the dullness of our minds
and give us the courage to comprehend
even the beginnings of possibility
if only we were,
all of us who call ourselves by your name
and others too,
if only we were
to give you that chance
for which you have waited
since before there was a time.

Help us to see
our place in your plan.

Lord,
make us the instruments of your peace,
where there is hatred, let us sow love,
where there is injury, pardon,
where there is discord, union,
where there is doubt, faith,
where there is despair, hope,
where there is darkness, light,
where there is sadness, joy;

So may your world be yours indeed,
your will be ours;
your benediction come
on all our living and loving,
thinking and doing,
to the glory of your name
and our eternal peace.
Amen.